MYRTLE'S STORY

A Dog's Life

Daphne Constantine

Daphne Constantine is a retired estate agent who lives near Ashdown Forest, East Sussex, home of Winnie the Pooh. She has had articles printed in several magazines and newspapers and spends a lot of time writing not very good poetry.

She has three children and six grandchildren.

Now in her seventies she feels she has finally found peace, having travelled all over the world. She enjoys history, humour, outings and the countryside and especially cream teas.

Myrtle was the love of her life, and this book has been written by popular demand from Myrtle's many fans.

Daphne Constantine, 2019

At Hever Castle, Kent, September 2018

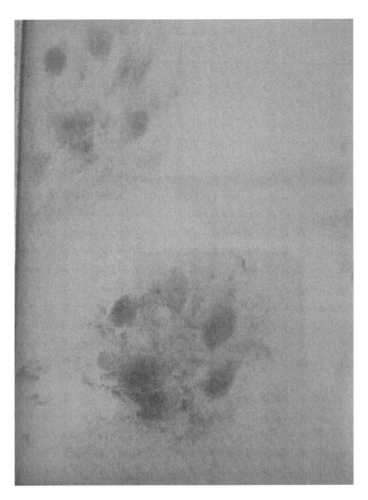

Myrtle's Paw prints

Dedicated to all those who loved Myrtle, from all over the world, from the Middle East to Australia, the USA to South America, Canada, South Africa and continental Europe, Russia,
The Far East
New Zealand, the UK. and Ireland

To family and friends

And Pekingese everywhere

"Until one has loved an animal, a part of one's soul remains unawakened."

Anatole France

Prologue

Pookie Before Myrtle

Before Myrtle came into my life In 2007, there was Pookie.

She was a black chihuahua X chin who came from Last Chance Rescue aged eight weeks and lived to be thirteen years and four months. She began my passion for black animals, but aside from the colour, bore no resemblance to the film star quality that Myrtle was to have, the charm and magic and gentleness.

Pookie was hilariously and preposterously inventive in her daily activities. She ate everything in her ambition to attain the size of a Rottweiler. She never got as big as our then cat.

She particularly loved eating carrots but she had to make sure they were dead first. So she would do her carrot dance. This involved jumping on the carrot and then rushing off at top speed in case it retaliated. She would creep back and dart at it and run away again until finally it surrendered, at which point she would roll on it to squash it to death. Then she'd eat it.

It was never safe to put any type of food at Pookie level. One day, really hungry, I put fish and chips on a plate, hot and mouth wateringly ready to be eaten. I walked out of the room, turned round and there was no fish on the plate. Pookie slept peacefully in front of the fire but on close inspection her breath smelled fishy. She denied everything.

Her personality was enormous. At our request she would lie on her back very still with her legs in the air and her eyes shut if we asked her to "die for England" but as she was so small that seemed too much to ask, so we changed it to asking her to die for "Tunbridge Wells" (which is a town near where we lived). She would happily "die" in shops, car parks or wherever she was asked to, to the huge amusement of the inhabitants of the town.

Her teeth were very originally designed and each took their own direction in life. Her legs were only two inches long and she had tiny delicate paws with little claws that made her look as if she should wear lace and smell of lavender. This was an incorrect assumption. She was tough and pushy and took no nonsense from any other dog, even one she needed a step ladder to threaten. She would sometimes just leap at the throat of some innocent passing giant canine, crashing to earth at its feet in a fury, just because it had momentarily locked eyes with hers.

She even stole the thunder at my younger daughter's wedding by coming dressed as a bride herself, accompanied by Percy my Japanese Chin who sadly died very young of heart disease.

Accompanying me to work one day aged thirteen, Pookie kept rubbing her eye with her paw. I casually wandered over to the vet with her at lunchtime. But I returned without her, following the visit. She had a tumour growing behind her eye.

My lasting memory of her was the night before, eating Thornton's sticky toffee cake and on the morning of her death sharing an egg sandwich with Karen, my work colleague, in the office. She seemed lively enough, but the vet's serious face, the knowledge of the pain and fear that would follow and my wish that she died happy, not afraid or suffering, made my decision easier.

That evening I went round to my daughter Melissa's and as she opened the door and our eyes met, we both burst into tears and hugged each other. It was the end of an era. There could never be another Pookie.

I dreamed of Pookie that night and that she could talk. She was in one of her furies and said to me; "Why on earth did you want to go and do that for?" I was terribly upset next morning thinking I had put her down too soon. A week later back she came again in a dream, this time looking smug and happy. "It's OK", she said this time, "I understand now. You did the right thing." I never dreamed of her again.

I still miss her, and smile when I think of her.

Two weeks later along came Myrtle.

Pookie always spoke her mind

The terrifying teeth with a life of their own

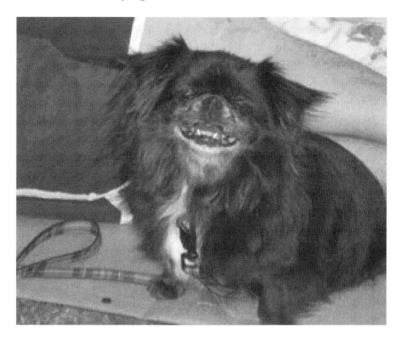

Pookie – individual, eccentric and larger than life

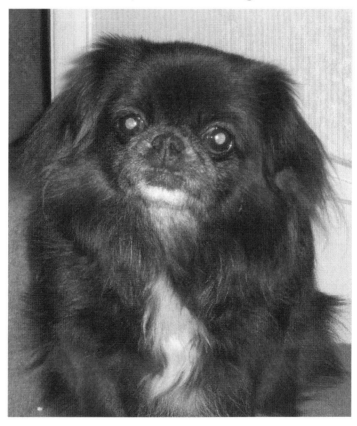

Pookie hijacked the wedding dressed as a bride, with her friend Percy as the groom

Chapter 1

Myrtle Arrives

All those years ago.... and a small hairy bundle of black fur waddled into my life. She was so furry that only her chunky little paws showed and her legs were invisible. Her tail curled like a black and silver fan over her back and her squished in little pansy face had big eyes, round and friendly, looking with curiosity and humour at her new home.

It seems now as if she was always with me but in fact she arrived just before I retired, at the end of years of bleak unhappiness, family deaths, divorce, illness and responsibilities that overwhelmed me. It was like struggling through a dark tunnel of treacle and at the end was the light and Myrtle. As soon as I took her into my arms that cold February night, I seemed to find a way forward, as if she was a guiding light, a guardian, something very special sent to me.

Myrtle was an eleven month old, stumpy legged, pink tongued Pekingese. A dog for an old lady or a little girl perhaps. A mobile teddy bear, a sofa dweller. Myrtle could have been all these and yet it was a tiny part of the huge character that she became.

She came from Whitchurch, in Shropshire. I think she was born in Sutton in Ashfield, Nottinghamshire. I bought her online without meeting her first. I cringe now to have done that in case she was from a puppy farm. I knew nothing of those then.

Her formal name was Zafirabon Moon Magic[1] but she was known as Poppy. She was black with a white chest and tummy and the tiniest patch of white fur on her chin. Her mum was snow white and very beautiful. I don't think Myrtle met her father.

She was chosen by the seller from the litter to be a breeding queen and was fifth generation Kennel Club registered. The seller then decided to go in for breeding pugs. War broke out between the pekes and the pugs and she felt she must make a choice to sell the pekes.

"Poppy" (Myrtle) as she was then named, appeared for sale on a website called e-pupz in the arms of a small boy.

Pookie, my previous dog, had died two weeks before, but the cost of getting Myrtle to be brought down to me in southern England by animal courier was a lot more than I could afford. In the end, after pressure from a bossy friend, I decided not to go ahead. I cried for days and then phoned the seller again to talk it through. She was delighted, saying that Myrtle had been seen by several prospective buyers but they just wanted to breed from her. She felt Myrtle would be an ideal companion for me.

The phone rang immediately afterwards and it was the animal transport company. The lady said she hadn't slept thinking of me alone and grieving for Pookie and offered to get Myrtle in the next few days for only two thirds of her original quote. I accepted.

---

[1]Well can you imagine calling me in at night with a name like Zafirabon Moon Magic? Id have run the other way! Myrtle

So she brought Myrtle to me one evening on a Tuesday in February, when it was sleeting and bitterly cold. When I opened the door, Myrtle was wrapped in a blanket with her little pansy face looking up at me. It was our first meeting and love at first sight. She was instantly Myrtle and never Poppy.

Her new name, unusual though the choice was, originated from the film Dinosaur, which showed in several scenes, a large diplodocus walking slowly along with a small black doglike dinosaur (an ankylosaurus apparently). Well, I'm pretty deaf and I thought its name in the film was Myrtle. I loved the creature and its name and vowed for six years that if I ever got another dog I would use it.

My moment came when Myrtle came to live with me and was proudly named after the creature.

Nineteen years after the film appeared, I discovered that I had misheard the name of the dinosaur which was actually called Url!   So I had been living a lie for nineteen years and Myrtle should really have been Url!!!! The name Myrtle sort of fitted, so Myrtle she became (and not Url).

I always loved dinosaurs. When I was about four years old I had a phantom friend, like many kids do, except mine was a diplodocus, invisible to everyone except me. I used to take it for walks on a lead around the cornfield at the top of my road and make my mother set a place at the table for it at tea time.[2]

---

[2]Spare a thought for me living with someone who had an invisible dinosaur as a pet before I came along! No wonder I'm eccentric.   Myrtle

It's very hard to sort things out at a distance and not meet the dog first.   That's what my daughter's mother in law got lured into - a rescue charity who home checked over here and then flew the dogs over from Greece. She'd asked for something small, fluffy and cuddly, maybe a Yorkshire Terrier. Off she went to the rescue to collect her pet.

The dog chosen for her looked quite dainty until it stood up when it was like a young giraffe, that unfolded its legs and stood about four feet high. She took it in happily and it towers over them and takes up the whole of the front room with a slightly baffled expression at finding itself in an apparently miniature world.

Myrtle was half grown when I got her. My two cats greeted her with loud purring, ran up to her and rubbed their heads against her. She had the same colour scheme as Pookie, so maybe they just thought Pookie had been away for a face lift.

Perhaps this early initiation into cat world confused Myrtle, because she greeted every cat she ever saw thereafter, with a wagging tail and joy in her heart. Her crestfallen expression when they hissed and shot up trees as she approached was obvious, but she never lost her belief that some day just one cat she met might reciprocate her offer of friendship. The odd one, dog conditioned, would approach her and even walk along with her, but she never equalled the relationship she had with Jaffa and Puffin, my ginger tom and white Persian.[3]

---

[3]Cats! Who can fathom their ways?   Myrtle

She would try again and again to interest Jaffa in a game. Jaffa, who was the John Wayne of the cat world, was unenthusiastic but would roll onto his back and wave his paws about. Unsure how to take this new unexpected move, Myrtle would sit firmly on top of him while he writhed and squirmed and finally escaped, only to return for more within a few seconds.

Working as I then did as an estate agent, Myrtle would, after some false starts, come to work with me and greet prospective buyers or sellers as they came into the office.

She peered out of the office window and many people stopped to look at her as they passed. Some even came into the office to ask about her. I felt she should draw a salary for enticing in potential clients but it never materialised. Usually she sat under my desk snoring. I loved the job and worked with the nicest people you could wish for, but I was a lot older than they were and my hearing was starting to deteriorate which made taking phone calls very hard.

Slowly the seed of prospective retirement started to germinate in my mind.

It was a fun job and had its memorable moments. After anyone had viewed a property I had to call them to ask what they thought of it and then report their remarks back to the seller.

Once we tried to sell a house right by the Gatwick airport runway. One man said he wouldn't buy it as he'd be scared his dog would be run over by an aeroplane. Another said when a plane went over he had hit the deck and covered his head. A third said that when a plane took off he could see the pilot's fillings as he grinned out of the cockpit window.

I like to watch the planes at night flying into the airport. It's as if they're all coming home, like living creatures returning to roost. I think Myrtle thought they were giant birds roaring at her.

Myrtle was a wonder to me since the day she arrived. For the rest of her life I found myself staring at her face daily, unable to believe anything so beautiful shared its life with mine. Her angelic huge baby eyes and sweet gentle expression were captivating but belied a shrewd intelligence and sense of fun.

She was very much her own animal, making decisions that suited her rather than me. This resulted in me frequently stumbling after her as she took off on some mission about which she had not enlightened me. She loved to be wild and free on Ashdown Forest, unsullied by human restraint.[4]

She was not trained to walk on a lead, but was mostly attached to one, clutched in my hand, and wrapped around my wrist, in case of her suddenly bolting off. It made not one whit of difference.

She devised a method of stopping, looking pathetic and refusing to move unless I carried her. As I bent to lift her, her engines revved and eel like, she would wriggle and run.

As a young dog Myrtle had a land speed record roughly equal to an Exocet missile. As soon as her lead was off she shot away like a greyhound from a trap and disappeared over the horizon, diminishing in size from a normal Pekingese to a small black dot in 0-5 seconds. Once out of sight, with me trying to run after her and whimpering her name again and again, she would go into hiding, cackling to herself at the fun of it all.[5]

---

[4]Wouldn't we all?   Myrtle

[5]I was just testing. Myrtle

Sometimes hikers would appear holding her under their arms, "We found this sweet little dog abandoned. Do you know who might own it?" Cue fluttering eyelashes and simpering from Myrtle, as I tried to be calm and wrenched her from their arms with a fixed grin. Or for a change she'd just lie under a bush, as dusk turned into night, while I wailed her name to the stars and received only silence in reply. Then tripping over her on my thirty-seventh attempt along the path she had disappeared along, I would finally be reunited with her, disturbing her sleep under a bush in the effort.

One of the worst escapes was one Christmas night. We lived in the forest on a very dark road with no lighting, and owls hooting in the trees. No moon or stars that night and my gate was across a water filled ditch. I hadn't been drinking either. Groping forward, holding Christmas gifts and with Myrtle under my arm, I slipped and fell on my back into the ditch, releasing her as I splashed into the water.

I clambered out, calling desperately for her as cars flew past. I rescued my slippers which were sailing in the sludge. I fished out my gifts from my daughter which were waterlogged and smelly. I ran up and down the road, covered with mud and slime, and looking like some horror movie apparition, shouting and yelling for Myrtle, to no avail.

I was terrified she may have gone deep into the forest or been squashed on the road. The total darkness, with no moon or stars and an irritatingly smug owl shouting instructions, did nothing to alleviate my panic.

I made my way desperately to my cottage and tried to phone friends for help with no success. My heart was thumping like a drum as I returned back up the garden path at speed, soaked to the skin, calling and hunting for about twenty minutes.

Finally, knowing she was lost for ever I returned to the cottage, pushed open the front door, which was ajar, and saw the little monster curled up asleep in front of the fire.[6]

Being black she was invisible at night. She must have passed me at some point going in the other direction, thought I was having a funny turn and gone indoors to have a snooze.

But I'm jumping ahead. Before those days on the forest was a more ambitious journey. No sooner had she come to live with me than I decided to retire and take myself and Myrtle off to live in Egypt.

---

[6]This is a most unfair description of me. I was being sensible while Daphne ran about looking like an idiot. Myrtle

Myrtle on right with her mum and sibling

Jaffa and Myrtle had great games from day one

Url, not Myrtle

Sweet Lila the Greek rescue

Chapter 2

The Peke that Crossed Sinai

"And the winner of the 'Dog with the Best Legs' contest is – Myrtle the Pekingese!" The judge at the local vet's dog show smilingly pinned a large red rosette on Myrtle's collar.

It was hard to see the thought process that had reached the conclusion that her short furry stumps were worthy of a prize, since they were virtually hidden by her fur.[7] However, to great applause from the surrounding visitors Myrtle sat on her back legs and waved her paws in time to the clapping. She had come a long way in the last year – literally. She had travelled all over Egypt as my companion and as far as she was concerned and many of her admirers, Myrtle was an intrepid explorer.

It had been another grey wet Wednesday afternoon in Sussex, watching the rain careering down the large display windows of the brightly lit estate agency where I worked, and I had had enough. My thumbs were getting arthritic and one foot was so painful that I felt like one of Dickens more picturesque descriptive passages, as I hobbled along. The silence in the office was interrupted by the occasional sigh from one of us, or occasional quiet throat clearing.

I noticed that it was five past three. When I had last looked at the clock about five hours previously, it had been five to three. I was sixty-two years old. Life was on the downhill run to the coffin. Surely there had to be one last swansong, something exciting that I could seize and do, and go out with a bang rather than a whimper.

---

[7]My legs are very beautiful like the rest of me.   Myrtle

Beneath my desk, a pig-like snuffling came from Myrtle as she snuggled down. My kind hearted boss let me bring her in each day and she enjoyed standing on her hind legs looking out of the window at passing children. She would crane her neck after them, making high pitched squeaks in disappointment that they weren't coming in to play.

I made my decision that evening. Just as the recession started to bite, my miserable, cold little house was sold. My mortgage, after the divorce, would have had to be paid until I was about a hundred and seventy-five. My children were happily living in places cunningly unsuitable for granny annexes. I was really on my own.

I decided to go and travel in the Middle East for a while. Friends and family regarded this as if I was voluntarily leaping into a cauldron and being cooked by cannibals. Myrtle turned big frog eyes up at me.

What was I to do with her? Many people loved her and offered her a home, with the hasty protectiveness of snatching someone off the edge off the cliffs at Beachy Head.   I anguished nightly over her fate. I decided she must come with me.

Myrtle, blissfully unaware of the turmoil, happily chased chicken on friends' farms and sat on any cats that approached her[8].

My granddaughter carried her around under her arm, like a fashion accessory and took her on swings, slides, even on an assault course at a dog show, though admittedly she did go under the jumps.

---

[8]What other purpose do cats have, other than as cushions? Myrtle

When the morning arrived for our departure, Myrtle peeked like a tiny furry goblin through the bars of her cage. Tied to the top was a label saying: "Please look after Myrtle and give her water for her journey," like a sort of canine Paddington Bear. I bid goodbye to her at the cargo department on the outer reaches of London Heathrow airport.

As we landed at Cairo the pilot cheerfully announced: "Welcome to Cairo and I can hear a dog barking in the cargo compartment." Such a relief! She had arrived safely!

I set off to find Myrtle in the minibus sent to meet me, careering around the airport road systems, stopping and asking various workers for advice as to where she might be. Most of them were smoking heavily and wearing leather bomber jackets and felt that their best contribution was to squeeze into the minibus.

I clung on, as we flew round corners without braking or changing gear and after three more hours chariot racing round the airport we ended up at the correct office. I was nearly on my knees, sick with worry, hungry and near to tears. Our driver returned to the minibus twenty minutes later.

"She hasn't left Heathrow," he announced sheepishly, "The customs computer broke down and she won't arrive for another twenty-four hours."

My head swam and my heart went into overdrive. Myrtle must have arrived in Cairo and been accidentally flown back to London again. Why otherwise would the captain have said he heard a dog barking when we landed? Or do hundreds of dogs fly daily to Cairo for holidays?[9]

---

[9] I felt like a canine Flying Dutchman condemned to roam the skies forever. Myrtle

That night I hardly slept in my Cairo hotel room. Back in England my daughter argued ferociously to find out the true whereabouts of Myrtle who seemed to have disembarked back at Heathrow and had now again boarded the plane for yet another ride to Cairo.

The following day it was confirmed she had finally appeared at Cairo airport. I paid heavy custom duties for her release. Unfazed, she wagged her tail and greeted the various men who had stuck with us throughout. I bore her triumphantly back to the hotel.

Staff emerged from hidden doors with mobile phones to photograph the fabled creature that was lost but now was found. Shopkeepers near the hotel who had heard of her story came to their doors to see her pass by like some canine dignitary on a progression.[10]

Our next step was to cross Sinai next morning. It took almost as long to negotiate Cairo's traffic and head south as it did to complete the journey.   Hour after hour of bland, flat beige desert lay before us, relentless and unvaried; mile after mile we travelled over it in the stifling, searing heat.

Myrtle settled herself onto my lap or the floor of the minibus and quietly accepted the curiosity she received at all stops en route. Small cafes nestled in the middle of nowhere where a light meal and coffee would be produced from very basic facilities. Myrtle waddled in and sat down, snapping at the bold flies which dive bombed her. "What is it? Does it bite?" asked adults and children, in broken English or by sign language. Within minutes they were bravely reaching out to touch her with big beaming smiles.

---

[10]I was. Myrtle

She gave only a cursory glance at the Suez Canal and the ships appearing to cross the desert. She also ignored, with contempt, the first camel we met when we reached the tip of the Sinai Peninsula. "It doesn't exist," said her expression and she walked past with a definite air of superiority.[11]

We finally staggered into the apartment which was to be our home. From one window we could see the mosque and from another the mountains. Here I intended to draw, paint and write and find some calm. I would swim in the pool at our complex, make new friends, learn Arabic and snorkel. At least that was the idea.

Egyptian workmen didn't work by the same clock as I did. Tomorrow might mean today, or more likely two weeks' time. When the washing machine flooded on first use, I initially accused Myrtle of weeing indoors until I realised the water was an inch deep all over the kitchen and Myrtle was floundering around in it. It turned out that the washing machine had never been connected.

Then the mice arrived. Myrtle spent ages watching for them to emerge from under the fridge, disappointed that they were antisocial, as far as she was concerned. They left in a huff when I put traps down. I never caught one.

The air conditioning was unusual. It was hit and miss if it worked at all but it was so hot that without it, being in or out was equally unbearable.

Myrtle had a cool bath each morning and even then once managed to dart outside and faint within two minutes. I was alerted by one of the workman. "Madam Daphne! Murchell shams!" (Shams meaning sun.)

---

[11] Well honestly, if you had to design an animal would you come up with a camel? Myrtle

I rushed out and scooped her up and dunked her under the shower and she recovered at once but after that I kept her indoors during the day and we went out at night for walks in the shadows and over the cooling desert sand.

My Arabic never quite reached the fluency I'd envisaged. The bus service in the town was basically Volkswagen blue people-carriers of dubious vintage. The idea was that you stuck your arm out as one hurtled up and down the main sea road and it would pull over and let you in. It cost mere pennies to travel almost any distance but you were crushed between sweaty workmen, smart businessmen, ladies with huge bags of shopping and babies. Dogs never travelled this way so Myrtle stayed at home or came in a taxi with me when we went out.

Anyway, the idea was that when you got to the place where you wanted to get off you yelled in Arabic: "Pull over to the side!" I studied the pronunciation until I had perfected it and with great confidence shouted it out on my first brave journey on the bus. Everyone on board burst out laughing and one woman was wiping tears from her eyes, her whole body shaking and her substantial flesh quivering as she shrieked with laughter. I got off thinking how friendly everyone was and what a sense of humour they all had, smiling and giggling as they made room for me to disembark.

It turned out that somehow my newfound linguistic talent had resulted in me shouting out: "I am a prawn!" instead of "Pull to the side!" Goodness knows how I managed that.

I never lived it down. Thereafter the blue buses became known as Prawns or Prawn buses in conversations with friends.

The Prawn buses were actually very dangerous. As you got off you might step into a hole, or on broken rock or uneven pavement.

Thus it was that my friend Ann ended up breaking both legs but being told by the Egyptian hospital that she'd just sprained her ankles. It was only after flying to Australia for a holiday a few days later that the doctors there x rayed and discovered the damage. Many weeks in hospital ensued instead of the holiday and when she returned she was wheelchair bound.

Myrtle and I would go each day to visit her in her upstairs flat, and Ann from a safe distance on the sofa would give me cooking instructions as I attempted to construct something edible for her.

In the meantime in Ann's flat Myrtle enjoyed sitting in the wheelchair when Ann vacated it for a more comfortable spot on the sofa. Of course Myrtle knew exactly where we were going each morning and raced off on the correct route past the swimming pool and up the stairs to Ann's apartment.

It took a very long time for Ann to recover and we were very wary of the Prawn buses thereafter.

In the meantime Myrtle thrived happily with very short fur and various visitors from England and new friends from the town and across the desert in Dahab. I learned belly dancing which wasn't much better than my Arabic and went to the market for fresh fruit and vegetables and finally joined an Arabic language class.

I loved the bus journey to Dahab through the desert. The mountains were never flat and grey but a changing kaleidoscope of colour through brick red, pink, terracotta, lavender and dark purple. Visible dwellings were few and people or animals rarely seen.

The bus would rattle and shake its way along the winding road, and visibility through the grime of the windows was often difficult. As it pulled up in Dahab, ancient pick up trucks designated as taxis would take you into the town. Either you sat squashed in the seats with the driver or you rattled about with the odd sheep or goat in the open back.[12]

After I'd had a giant ice cream, a look at the little shops and visited my friend Diane there, I would return by the same route and on arrival at the bus station would have a mile walk back to my apartment. Sometimes Diane would come to visit us and Myrtle and I would walk up to the bus station to meet her along the long straight barren desert road. We would see her in the far distance and Myrtle would strain on the lead to reach her, ignoring anyone else walking between.

I loved those warm evenings when the exhausting heat of the day started to fade and as night fell the stars began to appear in their millions in the darkness of the desert sky.

---

[12]Not with me she didn't.

Myrtle used to come to work with me

Myrtle the Intrepid Traveller

Crossing Sinai

Myrtle enjoyed sunbathing

Just the two of us in Sharm el Sheikh

Our complex

Myrtle preferred not to believe in camels

The Mosque at night

Chapter 3

Egyptian Days

Some days I'd take a taxi to the best place to snorkel and would slip into the silky warm water and float for hours watching the fish and the coral. Sometimes I would swim over what looked like fields of pink swaying grass like underwater heather as far as the eye could see in every direction. Whole shoals of fish would come up and swim with me over sea anemones and coral of every colour. It was such a busy world there. Shoals of goldfish that resembled the pet ones at home spiralled round and round in the sunlit water, down and down and down until the sunlight had gone and only darkness remained.

Often I swam in water so shallow that if I stood up it would only reach half way up my thighs but other times I ventured over the underwater cliff edge into colder deeper water with larger fish and a stronger current. There were fish of every size and colour everywhere. It was peaceful and silent and secret somehow. It was only when you ducked your face underwater that their world became visible.

From the surface, even standing in the water, you couldn't see the colours that clashed together like paint pots being spilled, as the scales and fins reflected the sunlight. I'd get out exhausted and dry off on a sun lounger before getting the taxi home to Myrtle.

For a change we'd take a taxi to buy an ice cream from McDonald's. Some taxi drivers were too terrified of Myrtle to allow her onboard but sooner or later a brave one would pull up and glancing nervously in the rear mirror for fear of attack, would transport us at twice the speed of light to our destination.[13]

Myrtle enjoyed these trips because she got to share the ice cream but also she was an object of intense curiosity as passers-by would stop in their tracks at her approach.

She reacted more than anything else to the strange, exotic and sometimes really quite evil smells as we travelled. She came into restaurants and even in one case, was stood up on the counter of a cafe so that the cooks and chefs could get a better look at her. So much for health and safety!!

Larger dogs were not a deterrent and Myrtle would frequently shout insults at the feral dogs which we occasionally ran into. At night, a lumbering pack of them would regularly run past our apartment at a distance in the desert, baying and howling. Myrtle would fly outside and stand with her paws up on the fence watching them. She made small excited squeaking noises and was desperate to charge after them - a bit like running off and joining the gypsies.

The dogs were sandy coloured and long legged and long tailed. There were five or six of them and in the rear ran a small black and white Jack Russell lookalike whose legs went ten to the dozen as they loped along.

I used to call them wadi dogs, as they lived and ran along the dried river beds or wadis in the desert. It was the only life they knew but often they came to grief and had terrible injuries when they were hit by a car, or when covered with sores and diseased they had no strength to search for food or water.

I got some strange looks when I spoke about "Myrtle and the Wadi Dogs" to friends, who thought I was referring to a pop group.[14]

---

[13]I always felt immensely satisfied to think I terrified enormous, unshaven, sweaty men in taxis. Myrtle

Nothing fazed Myrtle. She never exhibited fear and was quite startlingly intelligent, watching any animal programme on TV from start to finish, paws perched on the cabinet so she could put her nose against the screen.   She also knew the music of any advert which included a dog, even one as a small dot in the distance which no one else had spotted.

She would come skidding up to the television barking wildly as the music rose to a crescendo and she spied the dog minding its own business and ignoring her completely. Barking in a frenzy of indignation at its rudeness she would lurch from side to side of the screen trying to gain its attention, all of course to no avail.

Grown men shrank from her and were not reassured by my frequent comment that she had eaten two taxi drivers the previous week (untrue but satisfying to say). Mostly, however they were won over and "Murchell", as people pronounced her name, was definitely a celebrity.

The builders working on the apartments nearby were fascinated with her, rather in the manner of a rabbit watching a snake. They weren't sure whether to make fun of her or retreat rapidly from potential attack.

One new man who was six feet four and burly with it, was so overcome with terror at the sight of her that he leapt onto the back of the old sofa that the workers had dragged outside to sit on for their lunch and teetered there, ashen faced, as Myrtle and I approached.

---

[14]Don't go giving me ideas!   Myrtle

Ridicule from his mates brought him down with great tentativeness and when I held Myrtle in my arms like a baby and generally went through a pantomime to show how tame she was, he was finally persuaded to touch her, hastily withdrawing his hand afterwards.

Within half an hour he was holding her in his arms, a huge grin across his face at his bravery. Thereafter he was the foremost member of the Myrtle Fan Club, vying with the others to stroke her and pick her up.

I had brought with me a drawing of Pookie, Myrtle's predecessor, which was hung on the wall of the spare bedroom. When one of the workmen came into the apartment to do some minor repairs, he sighted the drawing and bowed his head in front of it.

"Murchell's father!" he whispered under his breath, before going and calling in his fascinated co-workers who adopted a similarly reverential position before the picture

"No!" I said, "Not Myrtle's father! It's Pookie! It's the dog I had before Myrtle."   They shook their heads gravely. "Murchell's father!!" they repeated like a Greek chorus.

Their respect for the patriarchal line meant that they couldn't countenance the possibility of it being her mother rather than her father and could see no reason why I would want a dog, which was not Myrtle's relative, to be in pride of place on the wall.

Thereafter Pookie, who no doubt was looking down from heaven in belligerent fury, was referred to as Murchell's father by any maintenance man or workman.

Our great good fortune while staying in Sharm was to make the acquaintance and later the friendship of Dr Albert Gabra and his family. Myrtle had been unwell as a result of picking up ticks and I was desperate to find a vet who spoke English.

My experience with the first vet I had found wasn't good. He'd offered to care for Myrtle while I was away for a few days but when I came back she had ticks and had lost her voice. He had tied her up all day or left her alone in a cage and she was furious and shouted for me to rescue her the entire time I'd been away[15].

Thereafter if I had to leave Myrtle I left her with ex-pat friends.

She quickly learned who was well disposed towards her on the complex where my friend Marian lived. Each morning Marian would open her door and watch as Myrtle did the rounds of the apartments, going up to a front door, behind which she knew lurked biscuits and a friendly reception and giving small yaps until she was let in.

Ten minutes or so later she would emerge and make her way to the next Myrtle-friendly door and so on until she had completed her circuit and returned to my friend's apartment.

One night after the sun had gone down like a giant orange dropping out of the sky, leaving the distant mountains lavender and pink like a great mysterious wall between me and what lay north, I put her on her lead and we walked three miles in the still heavy heat, past the mosque silhouetted against the evening sky, and along the road adjoining the desert to the surgery, which we had seen advertised in a guide about Sharm.

---

[15]Stupid man. I barked mostly to annoy him. Myrtle

A benevolent face and a wide smile were the trademark of our new vet. He picked Myrtle up as soon as we walked in and held her face up so he could look at her. "Hello Miss Myrtle," he said and Miss Myrtle she remained to him thereafter.

A highly intelligent, well-travelled and kind hearted man, passionate about animal welfare and adoring of his lovely wife Reda and his children, Albert was a wonderful person to spend time with.

Of an evening Myrtle and I would wander off on our nocturnal walks and often ended up having a coffee as he smoked the narghila or hubble bubble pipe at the cafe by his surgery. We would talk on all manner of topics long into the evening while Myrtle sat beneath the table people watching.[16]

Now and then Albert would ask us to help him. On one occasion a wadi dog had been knocked over and badly hurt and an Englishman had phoned Albert to ask him to go and help it.

Being wild it was unapproachable and was in any event surrounded by its pack, snarling at anyone who tried to get close.

---

[16]Its amazing how many different sorts of ankles humans have. Myrtle

It was on such an occasion that Myrtle proved a good decoy. Albert would drive us to the scene of the accident and I would hold Myrtle up to the closed window of the car. Galvanised into a screaming fury at the sight of her, the allies of the injured dog would abandon their friend and precipitate themselves at the car window, slavering and trying to bite their way through the glass to devour Myrtle. She for the most part coyly watched their antics, unperturbed and unimpressed while Albert darted forward, swiftly injected the victim, did what was necessary to patch it up and got back into the car again before the pack could see what was happening.

At other times we would arrive at the surgery just as Albert was performing an operation. Unconventionally, Myrtle would sit on the operating table as the animal began to regain consciousness, so that the first thing that appeared to the patient out of the mist and dizziness of a retreating anaesthetic, were two bulging eyes and a squashed nose a few inches from theirs.[17]

Some of the girls in the compound where we stayed spent most of their days in the pool and got the idea that Myrtle would be cooler if she joined them. This was Myrtle's idea of an attempt on her life. She hated to be out of her depth, refused to swim, sank like a stone, spluttered and struggled and clung to me like a monkey.

Once set on the edge of the pool she shook herself so rigorously it was like rainfall and after that she kept her distance from both the girls and the pool.

She would sit beneath the sun lounger far away from the pool, overlooking the distant jagged outline of the mountains and desert, with the acceptance of a well-travelled globetrotter. The Red Sea was just a big patch of water to her.

[17]How nice for them. Myrtle

The sun didn't deter her and she galloped over the desert with relish and trotted up and down the roads on her lead as if she had been walking in a Sussex park. She learned to love having a shower and to wear her fur short like GI Jane.

She was a good conversation point wherever we went and thus was the means by which I made many friends and acquaintances.

Of the forty odd somewhat casual proposals of marriage I had while we were travelling, some even included promises of a husband for Myrtle too. We both declined.

When walking her of an evening, people would catch me up and ask me how much money I would take to sell her to them. "A million pounds," I would say and they would look bewildered and surprised that there wasn't a realistic negotiating price. She was a commodity until they got to know her, not a much loved sentient being with a personality.

Myrtle became seen as an extension of me, and when I returned briefly to Egypt a year later, it was Myrtle that seemingly total strangers approached me to ask about. "We miss your dog," they said - which wasn't entirely flattering since they didn't mention missing me.

When our ten month stay ended, Albert and his family once again came to the rescue. He drove me, Myrtle, five suitcases of luggage; Myrtle's carrying box and hand luggage across Sinai to Cairo. It took nearly seven hours in stifling heat. Myrtle navigated from my lap.[18]

---

[18] I don't know how they would have got to Cairo without my map reading. Myrtle

We passed Suez and Port Said and crossed the Nile in traffic that came from every direction, appearing not to understand the concept of braking or giving way, until we finally reached Albert's apartment in one of the suburbs. It was on the tenth floor and the lift broadcast verses from the Koran as you went up and down.

His wife Reda had laid on a wonderful spread and his children eagerly greeted the famous Myrtle who they had heard so much about.

Reda and Albert's youngest daughter Veronica, who was only five years old, took a particular fancy to her. They even seemed to have the same hairdo.

That evening in the dying heat we did the sights of Cairo, Veronica holding Myrtle's lead as we browsed amongst the colourful bazaars. The people stepped to one side as we approached, like Moses parting the Red Sea. Heads turned, people pointed and gaped or laughed as the little girl walked along with Myrtle trotting behind her.[19]

Next morning we visited the Pyramids and Sphinx on our way to the airport. It seemed strange that Myrtle had seen so much in her short life, more indeed than many people. She had settled without any qualms wherever we had gone and with whoever we had met. Travelling was made common place for her because she accepted it as part of her life with me.

Before we had left Sharm to return to the UK, there had been an optimistic and unrealistic suggestion by one well-wisher that a fountain should be made with her statue on top of it and a drinking dish for dogs beneath it.[20]

---

[19]Are you surprised? I am after all a celebrity. Myrtle

[20]It is still a matter of deep abiding regret that this statue wasn't made. I should

It was a tribute to her compellingly magnetic personality that even in a land where black dogs are regarded as unclean and unwelcome, she had won over even the most stalwart objector and brought smiles and friendship wherever she went.

At Cairo airport it was over a hundred degrees in the shade. Myrtle was plonked in her cage unceremoniously in the middle of the melting tarmac by the officious man who took her from us at the cargo department. Albert quickly intervened, telling me sharply to remove her from the container and take her into the air conditioned offices nearby. The two men exchanged words in Arabic but Albert won the day. He said later that she would not have survived ten minutes left there in the sun.

We sat for nearly three hours in comparative comfort while she visited each office worker at their desks to say hello, before she was summoned by a profusely perspiring man, to be loaded aboard immediately or miss the plane.

I watched her tiny form hoisted up high on a crane in her little container and saw her swung precariously towards the dark warehouse as she peered down at me through the bars of her cage. It was the only time since I had left England a year before that I faltered and shed tears over her fate.

Albert whisked me round to the passenger terminal and I ran to get the plane, the last passenger on board and falling through the door just before they closed it.   "Is there as dog on board?" I gasped at the stewardess, desperate to know that Myrtle was loaded.

---

have been immortalised. Myrtle

The predominately English passengers, all typically animal lovers, overheard the croaked and urgent question and soon were all united in concern for the unseen canine passenger.

When the efficient stewardess bustled up and found me and said reassuringly, "The captain has confirmed that there is a dog onboard," a cheer went up. The excited lady next door to me grasped my hand effusively and we took off in a surge of emotion and goodwill.

We finally landed at a grey Gatwick airport five long hours later and Myrtle was unloaded and whisked off into quarantine without my seeing her.

After quarantine ended she joined me happily for a welcome home party with seven dog guests and lots of humans, in our old rented cottage in East Sussex. Here she led a very different life from what she experienced in Egypt, loftily bossing the wild rabbits and peering like a small watchful spy through the garden gate at startled passers-by.

Do I regret taking her with me to the Middle East? Absolutely not. She took each day in her very small furry stride and enjoyed every encounter with children and any new friends. She had a philosophical attitude to everything strange she encountered, from palm trees, to sunshine and camels.[21] She was with me, which was what mattered to her and she had shelter, food, water and lots of fuss – what else do any of us need?

Maybe one day we would tour together again, moving on like aging travelling hippies, but whatever happened, Myrtle and I were an item.

---

[21]Actually I quite enjoyed all the fuss.

Myrtle and I would walk at night time to avoid the heat

I tried out a hubble bubble pipe

The distant mountains turned pink and lavender as the afternoon drew to a close

Me with small furry tourist at the Pyramids

Touring the Cairo Bazaars

In quarantine

Chapter 4

The Cottage in the Forest

I returned from Egypt to England in November 2009, just before one of the worst winters for a very long time. It snowed until I couldn't open the front door and had to dig away the snow at the back to get out. While I took possession of the tiny isolated cottage on Ashdown Forest, in Sussex, Myrtle languished in quarantine fifteen miles away.[22]

I had never before been without an animal in my life and I felt very alone. Each day I would get in my old car and trundle off to visit Myrtle in her cold enclosure at the kennels.

On the way I'd pass cars in ditches where they'd skidded on the ice, cars overturned, cars crashed into each other, people slipping and sliding and others, more industrious, shovelling snow from their paths, usually into the road to make driving more difficult.

My old car never put a wheel wrong. Day after day it plodded on up to the quarantine kennels, sometimes in falling snow, always in compacted ice, but it got me there.

It was sad for the first few visits. When I got up to leave, Myrtle bounded after me, thinking she was coming with me and I had to shut the door on her, trapping her in her prison. It hurt my heart to leave her. However, being a buoyant and happy little dog, she just threw her toys about and sat observing the cats quarantined opposite.

Dogs round her barked and howled but she just sat there in her little knitted coat waiting for me to reappear.

---

[22]I've never languished in my life. Myrtle

Six vile horrible months of quarantine followed in thick snow and ice with her in a cage and run with a leaking roof and limited heating. I drove thirty miles in total almost every day to visit her and if I didn't arrive, the kennel maids would phone to ask if everything was OK. Some dogs had no visitors and no toys and just barked day in week out. My friends all visited her too and used to talk to the other dogs. When Myrtle left, her toys, which were so plentiful they covered the floor like a carpet, went to the dogs next door to her. I'd knit coats for them each evening at the cottage, and take to keep them warm too.

The following April her release was authorised. What a cruel experience for an animal quarantine was, not through the fault of the kennels but of the over zealous bureaucrats who didn't bother to consult knowledgeable vets to know that rabies injections work for three years minimum and Myrtle had had four injections in one year. In any event, simple tests after three to four weeks, even in those days, could clearly establish infection and yet six months was the timescale of detention for any dog coming in from a rabies infected country.

When quarantine was finally over the following April, Myrtle had a welcome home party with seven dogs and lots of humans[23], including the lovely elderly trustee and his wife who had been so good to me and had persuaded the charity to allow me to have the cottage to rent. Years later when he retired, his successors had a very different approach, and by then the ill health that was to bring me down had begun to bite.

While Myrtle had been away, aside from driving up and down to visit her, I had been looking after little dogs from the nearby area, whose owners were going on holiday. It was really to give me company and something to love and to take for walks.

_____

[23]It took me a while to work out that they weren't all going to be living with us at the cottage. Myrtle

The candidates were varied, from two tiny terriers who sat staring through the back fence into the adjoining farm, watching the chicken from the moment they woke up until bedtime - I called it chicken television - to sweet little Lulu the Lhasa apso, wonderful Mizbah the Bichon Frise and Oscar the adorable black spaniel.

Mizbah and Oscar started to visit after Myrtle had returned home.

Mizbah warranted a whole book to himself. Everything he did was at top speed, with enthusiasm, excitement and energy, from eating anything in sight to going for a walk. He couldn't be let off the lead because he would have taken off and got to Southern France on foot within four minutes, but he loved to sit on my lap with Myrtle sitting on top of him, so they both got cuddles.

He would always arrive pristine like a fluffy polar bear, glistening soap-powder white and perfectly manicured. Due to his rumbustious enjoyment of my unkempt garden and the nearby forest, he was regularly returned to his kind and warm hearted owners at the end of each of his visits, looking a strange mottled shade of grey with black lumps, food stains round his mouth and about four pounds heavier.

Once he even went back a vague shade of pale orange. My grandson Fergus, who was about eleven at the time, had decided he would bath him so that his returning family would recognise the dog they had left two weeks previously. Sitting with my nose in a book, I waved Fergus and Mizbah off towards the bathroom and told Fergus to use the nice shampoo on the side of the bath.

What I hadn't anticipated was him using instead, the self tanning lotion I'd bought.

After some time, which involved sighs, gasps, groans and loud splashing, Fergus reappeared, soaked through, with a bright orange dog peering out from a beach towel, held round it like a shepherd in a Christmas nativity play. Leaping into action, I grabbed Mizbah and screeching at Fergus to follow, rushed them to the bathroom.

It took us an hour to get the colour out and he still looked a bit tanned round his mouth and eyes. His owners were too nice to comment but Fergus, now nearly twenty, still refers to Mizbah as the suntanned dog.

Oscar the spaniel was a delight and Myrtle loved him. He was obedient, well behaved, a gentleman of the dog world. He loved his forest walks and every day we'd go for long stretches into the deserted parts of the woods and pathways with Myrtle bringing up the rear, like some Georgian heroine, daintily picking her way along.

She was especially pleased when Seamus the Westie moved in next door and she had two men friends to flirt with.

When I first got into the cottage I only had one neighbour, a tiny little old lady in her early nineties, all bent up a bit like the witch in Snow White. I was quite scared of her at first but she adored black animals, and loved Myrtle. She also loved the pop group Status Quo and played their music loudly most days.

One day I hobbled round to see her and asked how she was. "Oh," she replied, "I'm in a lot of pain with my arthritis every day but I just put on my Status Quo music and dance around the cottage". That image has never left me.

The almost vertical staircase in the cottage meant that Myrtle refused to descend it alone but would sit at the top, with her paws hanging over the top step, waiting to be lifted. Since she'd never once attempted the descent on her own from day one, this was quite an intelligent and considered decision on her part.

When she was content and sitting with me or any guest, she would grunt and snuffle and snort when spoken to. Then she would stop and let you reply and when you'd finished speaking, she would continue the conversation in peke language, sometimes long phrases, sometimes short, sometimes contented and sometimes outraged. This caused much amusement amongst my friends.

Living in such an isolated spot, one of my greatest concerns was what would happen to Myrtle if I died alone at the cottage and no one found me. Presumably after polishing off her roast chicken and biscuits she'd start eating me. Can you imagine the size of her if she did?[24]

"News headlines: "

"Giant Pekingese stalks Ashdown forest. People flee. Cars crushed.
"I thought it was a woolly mammoth," said Mr Smith of nearby Nutley. "My Rottweiler has had to have psychiatric help after seeing it."

However, somehow I managed to stay alive and the situation didn't arise.

---

[24]Such references to my figure are uncalled for. Myrtle

The forest had a magic all of its own. Home to Winnie the Pooh and the place where all the stories were written by A A Milne, it could vary in mood by time and season, from warm and welcoming and mellow, with glorious views towards the South Downs, to menacing and cold or threatening and haunted.

On some walks with Myrtle, I used to earmark trees to climb, just in case on the off chance, someone released an illegally kept tiger onto the forest, which saw me or Myrtle as a possible lunch. Despite the percentage chance of this occurrence in rural England being infinitesimal, it occupied my thoughts quite a lot of the time, whereas the more realistic threat of a mad person, rapist or human attacker never occurred to me.

In the winter the snow and ice were reminiscent of Siberian wolf infested forests, still and silent with no footprints but mine and Myrtle's tiny paw prints as we walked in the silence. I could easily imagine wolf eyes watching and a pack quietly creeping behind me. Of course Pekingese are, surprisingly, one of the oldest breeds and closer genetically to wolves than many other dog breeds.

I think Myrtle rather fancied the wolf connection and she also saw herself as a character from Games of Thrones. She never learned to howl though, so didn't quite qualify for an audition for a part in the Jungle Book either, and if she barked too loudly she scared herself and looked embarrassed.

As for me, animal lover that I am, wolves were just potential pets. At one country fair, a wolf was on show and for £1 you could queue up to touch it under supervision. In transports of delight, I joined the start of the queue, bursting through the gate of its enclosure and flinging my arms around it, kissing it and rocking it to and fro.

The wolf, which presumably had previously spent a life of quiet contemplation, being cautiously avoided by humans, looked shocked and taken aback. Its owners wrestled me off it, telling me it was a wild animal and hastily removing it to a position of safety. It peeked out nervously from behind the protecting body of its keepers and visibly relaxed when I skipped away, enthusing about my encounter with it.

I expect it had nightmares for months.[25]

Spring was the forest at its best. Walks down to Pooh sticks bridge with the blackthorn blooming like drifts of snow and primroses crowding the roadside.

Soon bluebells massed into blue and purple floral lakes under the trees and scented the air with a perfume impossible to replicate. Light green tree buds illuminated the forest paths. From the top of the forest you could see for miles to the north, the church tower of East Grinstead looking tiny on the horizon and to the east the towns of Crowborough and further towards Tunbridge Wells. Often I would walk up there in the early morning when the walks were wet with dew and Myrtle looked like a furry, misplaced giant bee pootling along ahead of me.

Summer in the heat, crowded with hikers, children waving sticks and shrieking, horses, birdwatchers, sightseers, cyclists clogging the road and blocking routes, was less of a favourite.

Cyclists in particular were a disappointment. So many shouted and yelled and bawled at each other as they rode past the cottage, regardless of the time of day, often waking me and Myrtle with a start on a Sunday morning.

---

[25] I have every sympathy with it. Myrtle

Many of them leaned against my front gate to mend their punctures, continuing their bellowing at each other as they did so and being quite huffy when I asked if they could move so I could get out.

Some decided to have picnics in our gated car parking area, throwing their bikes down and being abusive if requested politely to move outside private property. As an extra, many of the cyclists hurled their empty bottles and food wrappers over the hedge into the garden as they cycled by and left rubbish wherever they stopped.

On one occasion a family of five rode on the pavement over my feet without apology, as I sat waiting for a bus in nearby Hartfield and then, when I suggested they belonged instead on the road rather than the pavement, unless they dismounted and pushed their bikes, the father ranted and raged at my unreasonable request.

Another couple of cyclists, broadside on across the road on a bend, held a conversation and shook their fists at cars that came round the corner and had to brake hard, hooting at them.

Some would follow close behind lorries going up the hill to the top of the forest and hold on to the back of them get a free tow. It was the only time they ever seemed to keep quiet. Had a deer rushed across and forced the lorry to hit the brakes, the cyclist would have been mincemeat.

It was strange because the younger cyclists were almost always cheery and polite but it was the older ones who were from time to time unpleasant and confrontational.

Autumn in the forest was beautiful but somehow sad. Swathes of misty veils hung low over the dying copper bracken, ghost forms swirling and changing direction and confusing the distance and the way through. Giant stags would roam menacingly, antlers bristling and step without looking onto the narrow forest roads, hundreds dying annually as cars hit them.

There seemed to be something going with me and deer. One winter, I bought a clock with a deer picture on its face. Myrtle was eating her lunch when the clock threw itself off the wall, smashed the glass table top beneath it and then assaulted Myrtle by falling on top of her. She landed the other side of the room at the speed of a rocket from Cape Canaveral. She sat glaring at the dead clock for an hour afterwards while I cleared up the carnage. She took it very personally.

I always felt more uncertain on Autumn walks, muddy underfoot and broken branches barring old ways. I also used to get awful chest infections when I lived in the cottage.

Myrtle would look longingly at the world outside while I coughed and wheezed, unable to go out. Soon she drove her sick human to take her out after all, spluttering, and off we trudged outside into the gloom, every step feeling like lead through the cracking, dying leaves.

Collecting pine cones and wood for fuel and carrying buckets of coal for heating, made every day miserable. The sheer weight of carrying it, and the time used doing this to stay warm, was a constant struggle and one which precipitated the decline of my health into pneumonia, bronchitis and acute osteoarthritis.

However often the chimney was swept at great cost, the problems with smoke belching into the room were constant. Although quaint and chocolate box pretty, the cottages were not regularly maintained and tiles were missing from the roof and walls outside. The bathroom walls became black with mould, clothes in cupboards became musty and damp.

Once the fire got going, then the one sitting room became cosy and warm but upstairs you could see your breath in the cold like dragon smoke.

The fumes from the fire would sometimes become so acrid that my eyes would pour and I'd choke. I'd make a run for the door which led straight out into the porch and the front garden, Myrtle hot on my heels, and inhale the cold fresh air outside, snow, wind, hail, rain or whatever, anything to be out of the stifling oxygen-less atmosphere.   Up there on the forest the wind was like ice. It was like breathing glass.

I felt terrible morning after morning, wheezing like a steam train while Myrtle sat smiling very slightly, prior to her next Shakespearean rendering of a neglected dog needing a forest walk.

Strangers on the forest would stare astounded as Myrtle and I walked past. Hikers, perhaps down from London, weighed down with great rucksacks, would have been walking past farmers or countrymen with large dogs as they progressed. Horses and riders would have been evident. But the sight of me with my small Pekingese fazed them utterly.   Surely Myrtle belonged on a sofa, eating delicacies, not trekking the forest in all weathers, sticks attached to her fur, leaves adorning her tail.

Passer-by: what is it? Me: A furry hippopotamus.

The cottage had roof beams downstairs. The kitchen was a cold add on, an afterthought tacked on the back like a sort of reformed outhouse or tool shed. Off that was the loo and then the bathroom. Nothing had been modernised in years. Most things seem to have been ignored or bodged. The lower gutters didn't meet up and water crashed against the cottage wall whenever it rained. The upper ones weren't emptied in all the years I lived there.

I can't find words to describe the cold. The heater downstairs was inadequate and costly. Situated at the foot of the steep stairs, the heat just went straight up, leaving downstairs bitterly freezing. Guests kept their coats on in winter time. Unfortunately once any heat reached the top of the stairs, it wilted and died. The bedrooms were icy or airlessly hot.

The so called gardener whose job it seemed, was just to mow a circle in the middle of the lawn and then leave, once in a fit of over exuberant social conscience, announced that nothing had been done to maintain or care for the cottages for the last twenty five years.

Undeterred, I bought three hundred daffodil bulbs and planted them in the front lawn[26] over that first winter. I visited gardens open to the public to view snowdrops in February and bought varieties of all descriptions, tall, short, double, frilly and wild. These I planted in front of the window in a half circular border.

I bought at great expense, a Daphne bush and a Myrtle shrub, and planted them with beautiful old fashioned roses from the garden centre.

---

[26]I watched. Myrtle

Six years on, every single snowdrop, three roses and the Daphne and Myrtle were either dug up and destroyed or booted in near the car park, to die a week later, by the trustees who announced the garden wasn't neat enough, while I sat indoors with acute bronchitis. It had been such a happy place to live but I had become almost continually ill and upset.

Nothing could take away from me the happiness of the unique setting and quirkiness of living at the cottage but the time would inevitably come to once again move on.

Old and tumbledown but Myrtle loved it

Mizbah the day he became vaguely orange

Off on Ashdown Forest

The lovely old lady next door

On the forest in winter

and in Spring

Chapter 5

Ashdown Forest

At night in the cottage, the forest was a different place entirely. A cold crescent winter moon with a blue haze would hang like a Christmas decoration in the barren black branches of the trees, silhouetted against the threatening grey and black skies.

On other nights the blackness was so deep that layer upon layer of stars filled the sky, as if someone had thrown a million pieces of ice that shattered into sparkling points above. An owl would hoot; shadows would pass by; a herd of deer, a badger or a fox. In the mornings the plants in the garden would have been nibbled but the deer were rarely seen during their nocturnal visits.

At night, eyes always seemed upon you. You could explain away animals but there was something else, something older, more primaeval almost. A sense of the absorption of centuries of history, of it being untouched by the modern era and rooted back thousands of years. Were they Roman eyes watching, or Tudor, or ancient farmers whose story has never been told, long dead and forgotten?

The feeling was often palpable, especially with no artificial light to guide me from the car to the cottage. I would cling on to Myrtle as if she was some form of bodyguard, one arm outstretched ahead of me to feel my way forward to the front gate.

Only once did I come face to face with a deer. It was an autumn day and Myrtle and I were going to go by car to the top of the forest, so I strolled with her in my arms towards the gate.

As I approached the parking area I was aware of being watched. Standing right against the driver's door was an an enormous stag with huge antlers. He looked at me. Myrtle looked at him. I looked at Myrtle. We both looked at the stag. And then he turned and bolted, crashing through the undergrowth to escape the horrors of a small black dog held by a human. I think Myrtle was quietly proud of having scared him.[27]

The main claim to fame of the forest was of course the association with Winnie the Pooh. The author of the stories, his wife and son, Christopher Robin, had lived at Cotchford farm at nearby Hartfield where all the books had been written. Christopher Robin was shown in the illustrations as an old fashioned little boy with blond hair.

About forty years ago, I was walking on the forest with my three children, when ahead of us we saw a group of grey suited men holding champagne glasses and standing by some very large stones at the top of the forest at Gills Lap.

It turned out that one of the men, with steely hair and glasses, was Christopher Robin himself, who had come to preside over the inauguration of the stones as a memorial to his father and to E H Sheppard, the illustrator of the tales. Christopher Robin was then a fifty seven year old bookseller in Devon.

I don't suppose many people can lay claim to seeing Christopher Robin on Ashdown forest. We never caught a glimpse of Winnie and his friends though.

When I felt sad or worried or ill at ease with life and people, Myrtle and I would head for the forest and the peace and solitude. It gave so much calm and realigned my mood.

---

[27]Scared! He was shaking in his hooves! Myrtle

Often I'd get up at some unearthly hour to venture up to Gills Lap and walk along the high ridge with her trotting along ahead of me. At that time of the morning I was the only person there; the air seemed all mine, different, refreshing and giving. Great swathes of pink grass would ripple and sway smoothly in the early morning light like a strange alien sea.

Birds that normally hid from human eyes seemed to contain their fear as we walked quietly along. The nocturnal eyes had closed or turned away and there was no sense of threat or any feeling of being watched.

One of our favourite walks, usually with a selection of grandchildren, was the one to Poohsticks Bridge. Here children for several generations had thrown little twigs from the bridge into the stream below and then rushed to the other side to see which stick emerged first in the flow of water.

Even teenagers and adults enjoyed the fun. The original bridge fell into disrepair with all the footfall, and is now replaced by a copy, which is sound and just as effective. Myrtle found the walk there quite fun but it was a long one and coming back was uphill all the way, so usually I took her little buggy for transport. Sometimes dog friends shared a ride with her.

Crowds flocked during school holidays to visit the bridge to the extent that you couldn't find any fallen twigs on the ground to throw and had to bring your own supply. Sometimes the water got blocked up with twig dams from all the ones being thrown but it didn't stop the fun, or deter the visitors. At Pooh Bridge there was a connection, a link to gentler, happier, more innocent times, to a world unsullied by constant news of shocking violence, cruelty and war.

Local farmers had forest rights which mean their livestock could graze on the forest. This meant that driving along the forest roads could well mean encountering a herd of sheep having a snooze in the centre of the road or the odd cow standing looking disagreeable as you drove slowly forward willing it to move out of the way. it was worse when you were walking. Cows were known to dislike dogs and if they had calves would often charge any nearby dog walker. People had been trampled and killed or injured in the general area and being cowardly by nature I always avoided anywhere I thought they might be.

So it was on a quiet Friday afternoon that Myrtle and I got to the furthest point of our circular forest walk when ahead of us we saw three huge cows. No one else was around. It was me and Myrtle versus them. One was black with big horns, the second beige with white blobs and the third which seemed to be lying down was dark brown.

I quietly returned to Myrtle who was counting grass blades, her favourite hobby, and picked her up. I did a quick survey of the area. The cows were between us and the car. Either side of us was thick prickly gorse, bracken and trees. I decided that making our way through this would be a safer route than trying to either retrace our footsteps in case the cows chased us, or worse that we tried to edge past them.

So I stepped into the vegetation, catching my coat on thorns and my feet sinking into squidgy mud. Slipping as I crept forward, bent double so the cows couldn't see us, I held Myrtle protectively inside my coat jacket so the cows would not be goaded by her presence. More and more trees and plants made a grab at me and had to be unhooked or pulled off. My hair had twigs in it and a few large leaves. Finally we broke cover and were close to the car, the cows being behind us.

It was now that I looked round and was able to see that the cows were in fact a large burnt black branch, a large sheet of cardboard and a fallen tree trunk. They didn't resemble cows at all from that angle. Quite what I resembled as I burst out of the undergrowth and was faced with people getting out of their cars for a walk with their dogs, is another matter. Myrtle and I progressed to our car and got in with as much dignity as we could muster.[28]

Once we had warded off the cow threat, the sheep took over. There we were innocently enjoying a forest walk when I noticed large black furry lumps hiding behind the trees. A gang of sheep were skulking there, miles from any visible farm and were of course putting Myrtle in a risky situation by their presence because if she had gone towards them, any farmer could legally have shot her if the sheep panicked. I grabbed her under protest. Her whole life's ambition, she seemed to be indicating, was to cavort amongst the trees with a load of errant sheep. I beat a hasty retreat back to the car. with Myrtle doing her captured eel imitation.

On our way out to lunch next day there were the sheep again, this time staging some sort of protest in the road. Myrtle had only just recovered from seeing them hiding behind the trees the day before on our walk. Afterwards she needed to count a few grass blades to recover while the sheep presumably were spying on her using bushes as camouflage.

There were so many forest walks, and Myrtle loved them all. Tail up like a furry flag, she would, in her youth, lead the way along the paths, greeting all dogs en route with enthusiasm. Many people stopped to stroke her and ask what breed she was. Many, as usual, hadn't heard of a Pekingese.

---

[28]This is typical of what I'm put through. Myrtle

Not far from Gills Lap was Kings Standing. Here in the 1520s Henry VIII would wait on horseback with his attendants for Ann Boleyn, who he was courting at the time, to ride over to meet him from Hever Castle where she lived, to hunt the deer and wild boar.

Further down from the top of the forest height, was the original Roman iron foundry used for making weaponry right up and beyond Tudor times. It was said that Henry and Cromwell, his right-hand man, would ride down there some days to spend the afternoon watching the men forging the iron cannon, Henry thus escaping the cares and responsibilities of state. On such trips he would always greet people as he passed by with courtesy and warmth.

It's a shame we rarely get to hear of his charm and kindness and he gets turned into a pantomime figure chopping off people's heads.

Like most of us he had a good and a bad side but until he had a terrible fall jousting and was unconscious for two hours, he was generally a charismatic and well loved man as well as a good King. It was said that his personality changed after the fall and gradually he became paranoid and difficult.

Of course it wasn't helped by his need for a male heir to continue the Tudor dynasty after the civil War of the Roses that had devastated the land. To hold things steady, that male child was a must, but neither Catherine of Aragon nor Ann Boleyn gave birth to a healthy boy. Henry's panic increased almost month on month and on top of this, Catherine, his first wife of more than twenty years, was now past childbearing age and refused to have their marriage annulled so that he could marry Ann Boleyn and have the much needed heir. Sadly this was not the solution either.

It's hard for us five hundred years later, to understand the importance of his fears, and the way Ann Boleyn played him like a fish on a line until she became his rather disagreeable and spiteful second queen.[29] No doubt she was innocent of the accusations against her which resulted in her ultimate beheading, but the revelations were a shock to Henry when he was told of them and it is said he went pale when Cromwell told him. Modern thought is that Cromwell cooked up the accusations of treachery and incest to get rid of her, as she was, in turn, intent on getting rid of him. Whatever the truth, Henry had no choice but to act, or his paternity would be an uncertainty in the event of her becoming pregnant.

Myrtle of course didn't much care for these stories about the forest[30]. It was all just a walk for her.

The old Roman road often had sheep and cows wandering about so then we had to leave quickly in case one of the cows or bulls attacked her, or the sheep fell into hysteria at the sight of her and miscarried or fled and fell into ditches. When we walked along the road she always seemed to be counting grass blades and looking for Roman dog poo. I would walk roughly ten steps only on any walk because I was always waiting for her to finish some investigation or another.

Mostly though, the forest was clear of danger. Cyclists weren't allowed on the paths and horses and riders were usually courteous and aware of walkers and dogs and vice versa.

---

[29]Ann Boleyn had a small dog called Purkoy that ended up being killed by Ann Boleyn's enemies who threw him out of a window. I hope he haunted them. Myrtle

[30]This is true. Myrtle

The weather on the forest was unpredictable. We could start out from the cottage in sunny weather, me in a summer dress, and on reaching the forest, be personally attacked by a hailstorm, torrential rain or blistering heat. On some occasions we actually drove through the division between the two weather systems like a curtain, one side of the road wet and the other dry.

Myrtle loved the forest whatever the weather. She would sit for hours in our garden watching the insects and birds and occasional rabbit. As the fences at the cottage were completely broken down on one side, she frequently wandered into next door, now occupied by Joan and her West Highland Terrier, Seamus.

One summer I had my car loaded with Joan, Oscar the spaniel, Myrtle, Seamus the Westie and me. We had just enjoyed a lovely long walk across the forest in bright sunshine. We returned to the car and as we closed the doors there was a flash of lightning and the heavens opened, thunder, hailstones, torrents of rain smashing against the windscreen.

"Never mind," I said foolishly, "let's get home". I turned the ignition. Nothing. We sat there for an hour, mud sloshing round the wheels and relentless rain. We were a mile from home with three dogs.

Seamus, who used to have a nervous breakdown at loud noises, was shaking visibly as the thunder crashed and the rain bounced around us like some weather instigated apocalypse. Oscar, calm usually, was making whimpering sounds, looking sideways at Seamus, wondering whether he knew something awful that he, Oscar, didn't. Myrtle, invincible as ever, just sat there until Seamus began to bark and then Oscar howled, so Myrtle started to shriek.

All this cacophony of sound in a tiny car with thunder, lightning, mud churning and rain smashing down outside.

Then like a mechanical good fairy, a mud splattered car drove into the car park. It stopped nearby and two large dogs emerged with a man on the end of their leads. I climbed out and ran up to him asking if he knew about cars. He was foreign and didn't seem to comprehend why this soaking wet maniac had approached him.

Inside the car sat another man and a woman. I shouted for help at them and the man emerged, to be drenched within seconds. A quarter of an hour later, having lifted the bonnet of my car, he shook his head and gave up. Rain cascaded off his head onto his shoulders.

The lady passenger indicated us to get into their car. The giant dogs climbed back in looking cheated. The foreign man and his companion squelched in as well. Myrtle, Seamus, Oscar, Joan and I piled in, effectively soaking the nice dry lady and covering them all with mud. It was very cosy.

They drove us back to my cottage in their car, where I lit the fire, towelled off the dogs, changed my clothes and got Joan to take me in her car back to my abandoned one, in what was suddenly bright sunshine. My car started instantly. I was not speechless but what I said is unprintable.

Until Seamus told Myrtle that noises were terrifying things likely to kill her, she had always ignored thunder but after Seamus disintegrated at the sound of any loud bang, Myrtle started to tremble and shake at it as well.

Once she had taken Seamus's advice over the danger of loud noises, she went rigid with terror at any big storm, especially during the night. Consequently I would get to sleep some time after 4 am. But in the morning she would have forgotten the storm and be large as life, suffering no ill effects and looking at me as if I was being unreasonable as I drooped around with no energy for her walk.

The noise of one night's thunder storms freaked her out. I was terrified her heart would give out and in the end I think it could have been either of us that had a heart attack as the storm went on for so long, just like a bombardment of artillery.[31]

She spent the night under my duvet with her head on my hip and her bottom under my armpit, making wailing noises every time the thunder cracked across the room. After that Myrtle wore her balaclava to muffle the sound of thunder.

Pekingese may be brave little dogs but Myrtle was reduced to a trembling terrified jelly by a battery run child's toy hippo that roared and opened its mouth. Her smugness when it fell over was funny to see. If I lifted it up she would hide under a chair.

The front garden of the cottage was a permanent battleground in Autumn, as the dratted trees kept shedding leaves all over it and clearance didn't come within the brief of the so called gardener or the trustees of the cottage, so it was down to me and Myrtle to clear them, whatever the weather.

Raking them into heaps and stuffing them into our garden bin meant it was filled almost instantly, with ten times as many waiting to go in too.

---

[31] It might have been. How do you know it was thunder? Myrtle

It was a continual task, week after week, in sleet, frost, damp and cold and too physically demanding for me with my acutely painful shoulder and arthritic foot and spine.

No help was ever offered and sometimes I'd be crying with pain as I did it. The trustees told me to pay someone to do it for me. On a state pension? Not a very kind or helpful suggestion.

Seamus the Westie was a sweetheart and my neighbour Joan adored him. He'd come from a home where he was loved but not really properly looked after. His owner was a drinker who often forgot to feed him and finally Seamus was removed when the man was taken to a residential care home. Enter Joan. Within days Seamus was being given the life that a rescue dog can only dream of. A posh purple collar with spots and matching lead, a comfy bed, a warm fire to sit by, lots of walks and cuddles and chats, home cooked food and of course Myrtle next door.

Myrtle and Seamus were definitely Rhett and Scarlett, sometimes Laurel and Hardy but most usually David and Goliath, with Myrtle being Goliath. She would hurl herself at Seamus and shove him out of the way of the television so he fell with a clatter of coal scuttles and shovels into the grate.

She would fling herself on his back and leap around him while he stood stock still looking like a rigid four legged table, as if it was all a bad dream. But she loved him, really loved him. The words "Let's go and see Seamus," resulted in her flying out of the cat flap in the back door and through the gate to look for him.

Day after day they walked the forest together in all seasons and dear Seamus always waited for her to catch up with her short little legs and kept a watchful protective eye on her.

In hot summers they would lie together in the shade of the trees in our gardens and in winter they would conspire to edge Joan off the sofa, so she, not they, sat on the floor, while they watched the television in comfort. At the sight of Seamus or the sound of his bark, Myrtle's tail would wag until she seemed to have ten blurred tails. He was truly her very best friend.

Seamus had his fur cut and coiffured professionally every six weeks. On the way home with him after one such treatment, we stopped for Myrtle and Seamus to have a short forest walk. I looked back as we returned to the car surprised to see Myrtle walking with a strange black and grey dog. Seamus had leapt into the nearest mud hole and then rolled in manure.[32] Joan had the grace to laugh.

When Joan and Seamus used to meet us at the station on our return from trips to the Lake District, the reunion between him and Myrtle was always one of excited delight. Myrtle would fly down the platform and under the barrier to greet him, as Seamus strained on the lead to reach her. Both their tails would be blurred with the wagging while I struggled through the barrier with all the luggage and the pushchair.

Even after his death many years later she always reacted with joy when she saw a Westie like Seamus, running up to it and in one instance throwing herself out of her pushchair to say hello. But it was never with the total abandonment with which she used to greet the real thing.

When I moved to the flat in the village and left behind the icy cold, the damp and the difficulties that were the cottage, Joan moved too three months later, bringing Seamus with her to the flat next door to mine.

----

[32]Looks aren't everything. Myrtle

The day she moved, I took Seamus and Myrtle to the forest. It snowed. It hailed. It sleeted. It was face-numbingly cold with a screaming piercing wind. Seamus led the way straining against the lead, side by side with Myrtle who leant into the tempest, tugging me along behind them. They resembled intrepid polar explorers in Antarctica. It was me who made the decision to turn back. They were quite prepared to pioneer on into the blizzard.

Only three months after her move, Joan realised that Seamus was unwell. Over the next nine months he was gradually sinking fast into serious illness. He still enjoyed his walks with Myrtle but he was fading daily.

Then one morning Joan knocked at my door and asked me to come quickly. Myrtle rushed round too. Seamus had collapsed. He seemed to be losing consciousness. The vet came at once, even though it was a Sunday.

Seamus was put to sleep as Myrtle sat beside him and she watched him carried away in a towel to the vet's van.

Never again did she go to look for him or show any confusion about his disappearance. She knew he wasn't coming home.

Myrtle "wrote" a poem for Seamus on her Facebook page that evening.

RIP
My best friend Seamus
Aged 12
December 2004 – 4 December 2016

Seamus's Poem

Now I'm lying down to rest
Furry head on fluffy chest
People say it's for the best
And I'm too tired to care.
No more shaking friendly paw,
Wiping feet outside the door.
Hold me in your arms once more
And then put out the light.

The forest in summer

The Memorial to A A Milne and E H Sheppard creators of Winnie the Pooh

Myrtle and her best friend Seamus

All by myself

Our forest walks

Chapter 6

When Myrtle was Young

Myrtle nearly came to a sticky end a couple of times when she was small. Had there not been kind people around to step in and save the day this book would never have come into existence and she would have died horribly on each occasion.

Being totally trusting and expecting other people to have the same reasoning and thoughts and way of behaving, as the supposed common standard, I have found to be a grave mistake.

I used to tell my daughters that most people on this planet each have temperaments that are 75% nice and 25% selfish or not so nice. I reckoned that a small minority have a larger percentage of niceness in them, making them almost saint like and a similar group have the reverse, making them easily avoidable as they are so recognisably unpleasant. But, I warned my girls, the really dangerous people are the ones who are 50% nice and 50% nasty, as you can never read them accurately and never know which way they will jump.

When Myrtle was small I used to drop her off when I went to work, at the house of a friend of a friend, who claimed to love animals and made a great public show of fussing over my previous dog Pookie and then Myrtle.

When I first met the woman concerned in 2006, I felt a deep unease which I ignored, as my reasoning was that if my friend liked her she must be nice. Further warning bells rang as she had invited me for a blood analysis, which she claimed could predict illness or vitamin deficiency and then promptly told me I'd get cancer within six months. An unbelievably crass thing to say and one that could have caused panic or even suicide in some people.

I just thought she was a bit unbalanced and odd[33]. I never did develop cancer, which I am sure was a source of serious disappointment to her as things turned out in the end.

On another occasion I'd left an expensive watch at her house by mistake and hunted for it at home and in the car for days and was about to report its loss to the police, before phoning her to ask if she had seen it.

She had of course had it there all along but hadn't bothered to let me know. There were other small clues, things done or not done, body language, snide remarks, criticisms disguised as faint praise, intangibles hard to express, but I'm observant and read character well. She wasn't actually a friend to me or our mutual friend either, as became evident over the months when her behaviour revealed more of her true nature.

Myrtle was at this stage only a year old and teething, so a big passive aggressive attack on me took place one evening when I went to collect her from the "care" of this woman, who for brevity I shall call Lucretzia.

Apparently Myrtle had stolen her daughter's teddies to play with and had chewed one of the wooden stairs, though the tiny tooth marks would easily have rubbed out. Again, I thought this was a weird thing to bring up if you were caring for a tiny young dog and supposedly keeping watch over it but dismissed it as an aberration.

The following morning I drove four miles over to her house as arranged, to drop Myrtle off before work, but the house was empty and no one answered, despite her having told me that she would be there.

---

[33]Now she tells me! Myrtle

I waited and waited until I was late for work and then with Myrtle still with me, drove to the office. Lucretzia arrived just behind me and took Myrtle, with no apology or explanation as to why she hadn't been at her house as promised; presumably she'd taken her daughter to school late.

During the morning my boss was out and I was manning the office alone, when the phone rang. "Do you own a small black dog?" said a man's voice. I replied that I did. "Well I've just found it running in the traffic. I've got it in my car". I asked him to return Myrtle to the address nearby where Lucretzia lived. He rang back and said there had been no reply but he'd popped Myrtle in through the cat flap. I tried repeatedly to phone Lucretzia on her landline with no answer. Feeling thoroughly disturbed, I decided to go and fetch Myrtle at lunchtime.

Within seconds however, the phone rang again. This time it was a woman. "Are you the owner of a black puppy?" I said I was. "Well my daughter has almost been knocked over by a van, running into the road to stop the dog from being killed." I explained Myrtle was being "looked after" by Lucretzia and gave the address. "Well, I'm not going anywhere until either you or she comes and personally takes this little dog," said the woman. I couldn't just desert the office, so I rang Lucretzia, this time on her mobile phone and the following explanation from her ensued:

"I'm VERY angry! I was meeting a friend for lunch today in Tunbridge Wells and when I started to drive off, Myrtle came out of the cat flap and chased my car! I tried FOUR times to make her stay indoors but she just followed me, so in the end I just LEFT her and DROVE off. And NOW you're asking me to come home to fetch her from this woman?" This, as you may imagine was the end of any so called friendship between us.

Lucretzia returned home from Tunbridge Wells, took Myrtle from the woman who had loyally sat with her until she arrived, and then Lucretzia drove Myrtle back to my house, where she dumped her and my front door key.

The woman rescuer rang me again about an hour later. I thanked her profusely for her kindness and help and asked if I might have her address to send her some flowers. "I don't want flowers," she said, "I just want a promise from you that you will never leave your little dog with that awful woman again. Her own dog was running around the dustbin lorry unchecked while she was talking to me and she was thoroughly resentful and spiteful about having to curtail her outing". I made the promise she requested.[34]

Sadly Lucretzia also made sure my friend, who was our mutual contact, was told how she had made "a mistake" and "after all she'd done" to help me with Myrtle, I had been angry at her for what had happened. And so ended that friendship as well.

Lots of things then returned to my mind. How many people had said to me that Lucretzia "arranged her face into a sweet smile" when anyone was watching her, but when she didn't think they were watching, a dark and nasty look came over her features. How she had stopped working on the grounds of illness and spent months sunbathing and out shopping despite pleading poverty, while receiving benefits including concessionary foreign travel, from her employer, yet having no obvious intention of returning to the job. How her constant stories of financial hardship and being in grave debt didn't make sense, bearing in mind the offer of two very easy morning only part time jobs offered to her, via me, from people I knew in the local town, which she turned down out of hand "I am NOT giving up my travel concessions," and so on.

[34]Thank Goodness for that. Myrtle

It was a sad lesson. Her character was self seeking, quietly spiteful, deceptive, manipulative, mendacious and mercenary and yet she could be charming, amusing and persuasive. A frightening mixture.

My boss was absolutely appalled and furious when he returned to the office that morning and heard what had happened. "Myrtle is to come into the office with you every day," he said, red in the face and eyes blazing. "That woman is irresponsible. She lies through her teeth, courts sympathy from everyone and does exactly what she likes. She must never have the care of Myrtle again."

As time progressed further reports of Lucretzia's two faced actions or custom built explanations for her deficiencies in life, filtered through, none of which seemed to tally with each other. She was definitely one of the 50% nice 50% nasties that I went on to warn my daughters about.

And so henceforth Myrtle became the office mascot and came in with me to work. She behaved beautifully and never again spent any time with anyone other than me on working days. For holidays I paid a neighbour from when I was in my twenties, who was a professional dog carer, and Myrtle had a good time organising the other guest dogs.

My old school friend friend Barbara who has lived in New Zealand for nearly fifty years comes over to stay with me regularly and enjoyed days out with me and Myrtle. We decided on one outing, to go for the day to the seaside and visited a place on the south coast of England called Beachy Head, huge chalk cliffs overlooking the English Channel with the rough sea crashing against their base. Many dogs run and play up there happily without incident, so I took Myrtle's lead off so she could have a trot about.

As soon as the lead was released, she took off like a guided missile heading straight for the cliff edge. Barbara and I panted after her, gasping and croaking her name. She nipped and dodged round people trying to catch her, with all the determination of a rugby player about to score a try. She was finally intercepted by a young man who flung himself bodily on top of her. We staggered up and prised her from his grasp.[35]

Never again. I later discovered that it is a well known accident black spot for dogs. One chased a frisbee over the cliff edge and crashed to its death on the rocks below.

I learned my lesson in those days but I could have have lost her for ever and it would have been my fault for not seeing the danger. I still shudder to remember it.

You know - it's very odd the way we learn lessons in life. The number of times I'd taken her for walks and let her off the lead and she'd never made a break for the border and then when at risk in a situation which was potentially fatal, she took off like a motorbike.

Myrtle loved peacocks and parrots. She didn't chase or hurt them but sat riveted by them, watching their every move. A friend had a parrot called Henry, and Myrtle spent hours watching it while it said: "Hello babe!" to her and danced on its perch. We sometimes saw some peacocks at the nearby llama park. They looked in the windows while we were having tea. Myrtle thought they were greeting her and whenever we visited searched for them to say hello. The llamas didn't interest Myrtle at all.

Myrtle had a personal vendetta against pigs, particularly toy ones from IKEA. She went through eight in two years and never rested until they were cowering and subdued.

[35] I had intended to stop at the edge anyway. They just panicked. Myrtle

I had a pig store in the cupboard. When IKEA seemed to stop selling them I was in need of CPR. Fortunately I found one in a charity shop and then they reappeared in store. I would bulk buy them, three at a time in case they disappeared again. The shop assistants must have thought I was some funny old obsessive woman who had a thing about identical toy pigs.

Myrtle went through the pigs like a whirling dervish, ripping them to bits and spitting the stuffing out in fluffy lumps when she was sure they were dead and disembowelled. No other toy brought out such ferocity in her.

Her love affair with spiders began when we moved into the cottage. Spiders had been in residence for many generations and were probably put out by my arrival.

Since I can't bear to kill living creatures but am terrified of eight legged ones, I would put a glass over them to stop them galloping off and then carefully slide paper underneath and turn the glass the right way up. The spider then was hurriedly thrown over next door's fence. Some of them relentlessly plodded back. In fact I recognised them on their return because they were so large that their facial features and expressions were familiar.

I read an advertisement that having conkers in the house from a horse chestnut tree, were a sure spider deterrent. I collected a large carrier bag full of them and lugged it back to the cottage. There were conkers along the mantelpiece, on shelves, along the skirting board, in vases, alongside ornaments, down the back of the sofa, in the kitchen, in every cupboard, along the side of the bath and on every windowsill. They were lined up along the doorways and suspended on strings from the beams.

I took them all down when I discovered a spider of enormous proportions happily settling down on top of a pile of conkers on the mantelpiece, with a nice web in and out of the conkers and what may well have been a smug smile on its face.

When Myrtle got out of quarantine and returned to the cottage, the spiders' presence gave her undiluted joy. I always knew when there was one in the room because she would leap to her feet, tail frantically wagging and dance up to it wanting it to play. A new friend! This is great! Can he stay for tea? She never hurt them and would sit fascinated watching them until I evicted them.

Sitting outside at a tea room one Spring, suddenly she was pulling hard on her lead and knocking chairs sideways. No dogs in sight. No cats. No children. All these she would gladly have joined up with. There was the tiniest little spider walking along minding its own business but irresistible.

One morning I had to call in a Man to mend the television. Myrtle would have given up the ghost if she couldn't shout abuse at the adverts and drown out any programme that interested me if she saw a dog in it. Naturally she wanted to check the man was mending it properly and also to advise him on the best way of doing so. She elbowed her way forward so she could watch what he did for future reference. She did like to help.[36]

From the moment he arrived until he packed up and was on his way she dogged his footsteps, glancing at him confidingly as he produced various screwdrivers and electronic testing devices, as if she understood perfectly what he was doing. Fortunately, he explained to her and included her in the procedure. When he finally left she visibly sighed and settled down happily for a snooze, exhausted with her efforts to help.

[36] I am generous with my talents. Myrtle

I don't think Myrtle realised she was a dog. She just thought she was a unique being and should be the star of every show. She had no defence mechanism towards humans, just expected them to include her. She'd have held the torch for the burglar if one came.

She preferred to be a front seat rather than a backseat driver. Her favourite position was with her bottom hanging into the back of the car between the front and back seats and her head and front paws neatly fitting between the two front seats. For a change she liked to balance precariously on the handbrake which could hardly be comfortable.

Her most extraordinary position was with her bottom on the lap of the front passenger and her body suspended in the air between the front passenger and driver's seat with her front paws and head teetering on the edge of the driver's seat. For changing gear, it was necessary to negotiate a furry pair of ears or a head or nose. So she was banished to a restraining harness in the back where she would sit rock still, sulking at not being able to either drive or navigate.

Despite the sweetness of character oozing from her whenever anyone stopped to talk to her, she couldn't always be relied upon to love every dog she met with the same enthusiasm. Just occasionally she took one look at an innocent oncoming canine and decided it was probably a mass murderer of Pekingese. Obviously it was down to her to protect the species. Regardless of its size it had to be defeated, squashed, flattened and sent on its way with as many fleas in its ears as she could enrol.

Often the victim fled on sight as Myrtle hurtled menacingly towards it. On the odd occasion it puffed itself up to fourteen times its original size and rearranged its face into one of threatening loathing.

I don't know if Myrtle was short sighted or if she just didn't care but she never flinched or faltered and thus I and the intruder's owner would be forced to wrestle them apart and drag off our screaming pets on their walk, still shouting insults at each other.

She only ate if hand fed, (after about a quarter of an hour of turning away and pretending to be disinterested). This entailed my 85 year old neighbour lying on her stomach trying to tempt her with morsels from a plate. I refused to do this until Myrtle was in imminent danger of starvation when I too capitulated. Lamb was her favourite, freshly cooked, or turkey or chicken breast or fresh poached salmon all mixed with a variety of vegetables, home cooked.

Sometimes absolutely nothing appealed to her delicate palate. She never liked treats or chews, and looked cheated and neglected if cakes, biscuits and human food weren't shared with her.

Should anyone have arrived for tea, she stared pathetically up at them with big tear filled eyes, trying to project the fact that she was hardly ever fed and needed whatever they were eating, I had visions of her drifting about like a starving waif, rolling her eyes at passers by and eating the bread for the ducks.

Myrtle backed away from bone china as if it had germs and hadn't been washed properly and when, pouring sweat and exhausted, I walked in having cooked her a meal, she glared at whim at roast beef as if it was dead rat[37]. She had a way of making me feel an inadequate and useless mother and cook.

---

[37]It may well have been. Myrtle

She would search relentlessly for a whole walk for a suitable place to wee, turning round and round at the chosen spot and then changing her mind and walking on and going through the same performance again. Her longest periods of indecision were in snowstorms or torrential rain. Accidents indoors were unheard of, bar two occasions, once when she was ill and once when she was shut indoors for longer than anticipated. Both times she went into our bathroom and did it next to the loo which I thought was very clever.

I spent most grooming days with Myrtle perched on the draining board in the kitchen while I shaved and cut all her fur off because of the heat. Hence next day the temperature would drop and she'd be frozen, so I had to hunt round for a sweater I had knitted her years ago one winter. She seemed happier with it on than without it but I'm not sure if that was due to the cold or the look of the haircut.

I indulged in my secret desire to be a hairdresser in my grooming attempts but when I gave Myrtle an ear cut as her fur was hanging in her food, the result meant that I shouldn't give up the day job if I had had one. The problem was that I couldn't get them even. I'd snip off a bit of one and then it looked shorter than the other, so I cut off a bit of the other ear and so on and on and on until her ears were titchy little things and her face looked like a seal. She glared at me as if she had just been scalped.[38] If anyone called her GI Jane amidst shrieks of laughter she looked quite pained and would sulk. Red bows didn't make it better either. Possibly a hat would have disguised her shame.

---

[38]It defies belief how anyone could have done this to me accidentally. It must have been deliberate. Myrtle

Myrtle sort of grew into her new ear haircut. My daughter thought she looked cute and the grandchildren giggled. Lots of passers by commented on Myrtle's original look and wanted to stroke her but as usual had never heard of the Pekingese breed.

Bath time for Myrtle was not her favourite past time. From the first assault on her person to the final release she was astounded that anyone could do anything so mean and pointless. "I suppose you think that was funny," said Myrtle after a bath. She had a sense of humour bypass when faced with washing or (usually) rain.

I noticed how many other dogs had big smiles and looked happy and full of fun. Myrtle seemed to have, like me, an expression which looked as if the world had just ended. It's particularly noticeable in photographs of her with dog friends. There they are with a lovely doggy smile and Myrtle's mouth is turned down so far it almost touches her paws. It reminds me of those theatrical masks where one is smiling and the other looks miserable. It was her default expression. As I always look miserable too, people are always telling me to cheer up when there isn't anything wrong. Myrtle and I just looked like that normally.

The "Dog with the most beautiful legs," was a title that somehow didn't fit Myrtle's persona and yet it was when we returned from Egypt and attended the local vet's dog show that she took away this esteemed prize. She had a rosette to prove it. But it wasn't the end of her prize winning successes.

Another time she was pushed down to the vet for the dog show in her stroller because it was very hot and she couldn't walk far. She got first prize for The Dog with the Softest Ears. It turned out she had also won Best In Show[39] but we had already left before the announcement as it was so hot. So what with soft ears and beautiful legs we then hoped for a prize for the bits in between, like her face or her fur.

Of course since we lived on Ashdown Forest many of our days were spent walking along the forest paths through the prickly gorse and along the ancient tracks high on the Wealden ridge. In distance we could clearly see the South Downs, the other side of which is the English Channel, and fifteen miles across that is France. So we were nearer to France there than we were to say, Liverpool or even a bit North of London probably.

Myrtle loved those walks, running free or sitting on a bench beside me looking at the blue tinged misty views. Now and then huge dogs with energetic owners would speed past and I felt a slight sadness that the owners' wish to rush everywhere meant that they never stopped to look around them at the beauty.

---

[39]Obviously. Myrtle

She was the perfect size to hold and cuddle for a woman living alone. Roughly the size of a human baby with the same out of proportion huge round eyes, cuddly as a teddy, as easy to care for as a cat. Every night I would carry her upstairs in the cottage and put her on my bed to sleep. Often she would curl up on the pillow next to me, snoring happily. Far from being an irritant those snores lulled me to sleep. They had something of the purr of a cat, the rhythm of gentle breathing, soothing and calming. Before I slept I always spoke the same words to her: "Goodnight my beautiful girl, I'll see you in the morning. Mummy loves Myrtle. Night night my sweetest Angel". Writing it sounds silly and sugary but it was a mantra, a gratitude for her company and her magic, a charm to keep her alive for ever and ever and never to leave me.

Myrtle's childhood passed quickly with my retirement, Egypt and then quarantine but her time at our cottage was probably the best of her life. There she was happy and free in a big garden full of interesting things to watch and listen to.

She flew off on her forest walks, enjoying the sun on her back and the wind in her ears. Every day was an adventure and a joy for her, and for me watching and being with her.

The forest seemed our spiritual home, our natural place to be.[40] When we were there together life seemed complete and all the difficulties and worries of the world and everyday existence fell away.

---

[40]I'll always be there for ever and ever. Myrtle

Myrtle at about a year old

Pass the parcel with the grandchildren

Winner of the dog with the softest ears competition

Travelling with a friend

On the forest

Lurking sheep

Always beautiful - Ashdown Forest

Poohsticks Bridge with friends

Chapter 7

Off on our Adventures

Myrtle and I were always off out somewhere. I never was a stay at home person. There's a lot of world out there. Myrtle would sit and stare steadily at me of an afternoon willing me to stand up and get her lead so we could go out in the car.[41] So she was well travelled.

She had flown with KLM airlines to Egypt and had of course seen the Pyramids and the Cairo bazaars; she had climbed Hadrian's Wall in the north of England; she went on planes, trains, buses, taxis, cars and boats; saw the Red Sea and crossed the Sinai desert.

I would have loved her if she had done nothing and gone nowhere but we had such great adventures. She was a magical little thing and I felt so lucky to have shared her life. I will treasure my times with her always. She truly changed my life. With Myrtle I was never alone.

The Internet has its critics but through joining various groups dedicated to Pekingese, Myrtle and I came to meet some very kind and wise people from all over the world.

Some of them came to visit us and became good friends, while others became pen friends and a shoulder to cry on when Myrtle's health was bad or everything started to overwhelm me.

---

[41]Daphne was hard work sometimes. Myrtle

Thanks to Myrtle and her admirers in the UK, USA, Canada, Argentina, all over continental Europe, Russia, New Zealand, Australia, South Africa, the Far East and even the Middle East, I came to realise that what I had always believed was true; your average human being is well intentioned, good hearted, has a sense of humour, wants to help and cares about others, no matter what their nationality.

In all the years we belonged to these groups both of us knew nothing but concern, praise, kindness, sweet messages, good advice, suggestions and encouragement. There was one self involved exception, who caused unpleasantness for a short time but she was a totally isolated instance. There's always one bad apple.

Myrtle had a large following of people who genuinely loved seeing her photos and hearing her adventures and expeditions. Others we met on the course of our walks opened our eyes to the friendliness of people and the love of animals that was almost as instinctive as loving their own human children. Dogs are to most people, adored family members that just happen to look a bit different.

The similarities between ordinary human beings in terms of kindness and caring for others, takes me back to when I'd taken my three children to Belgium on holiday. My son Nick was twelve, tall, blond and blue eyed. We went into a shop and a very old lady was making lace. Her daughter explained in English that her mother was the last person to be able to make this particular design and that when she died the knowledge would die with her.

At this point the old lady looked up and held her arms out to my son, speaking rapidly in her own language. Her daughter translated: "My mother says he looks so like the young British boys who came and helped Belgium during the wars."

The old lady brought my son close to her and hugged him with tears in her eyes and then turning to her work, cut a piece of the lace she had been weaving.

"Thank you! Thank you!" she said in heavily accented English.

My son was somewhat bewildered at why she was thanking him. A few days later when he saw so many Commonwealth War Graves in multiple cemeteries, and so many headstones for 18, 19 and 20 year olds, he started to understand. I kept the lace for many years until it disappeared in one of our house moves.

The grandchildren were also fans of Myrtle. She always wanted to join in their games and especially liked to think their birthday parties should revolve around her. Thus the game Pass the Parcel had to include her and she was quite happy to be dragged along on her lead for a walk if one of them was in charge, whereas she'd have sat down if it had been me. She would run out in the garden with them to the paddling pool, or enjoy a cartoon with them on television.

December was quite an eventful month for me and Myrtle each year for some reason. There was the year a deer wrote off the car I'd only been driving for just over a week, my iPad seemed to get dementia and kept doing weird things and finally stopped working and then Myrtle went to the vet. She had stopped eating and could only be persuaded to nibble anything if I pretended to eat her food myself. Even then it was half hearted and she spat bits out.

Alex seemed to be baffled and looked at me as if I was making excuses to visit him. Myrtle happily watched the News on television that evening, just to show that her superior intellect had no time for lesser things like eating.

The deer had deliberately attacked the car by jumping onto it from a bank at the side of the road, crushing it, and then had gently slid off it onto the tarmac, from where it managed to kick and head butt the car until it wasn't fit to drive. It then walked off placidly and munched grass at the roadside as if I, the car, and my weeping neighbour were of no consequence whatsoever. Fortunately I had been driving slowly, hence the survival of the deer on impact.

Myrtle wasn't in my car when it was written off but I think she smelled the deer because some of its fur was stuck in the car radiator and then when she realised the car couldn't take her out any longer, she put two and two together and realised this nasty smelling creature had murdered it.

She seemed to be very affected by the absence of transport and her daily forest walk. Moping indoors and yawning when I suggested a walk down the footpath near where we lived, until another car was procured, with kind financial help, a couple of weeks later.

Sometimes deer tried to hide incognito among herds of sheep in fields, thinking that being hidden in plain sight made their presence unseen. A couple of times since the car murder they appeared in the forest and Myrtle gave them witheringly baleful stares that would be envied even by an obelisk. They sensibly fled. Myrtle's Christmas outfit the next year was a headband with reindeer antlers to reinforce my day dreams of scaring off the next deer I met.

Christmas Day and turkey was usually at the local pub, with my daughter and family and of course Myrtle came too, with festive red bows in her ears. The place was full of dogs, large, small, fluffy and smooth haired.

Myrtle was fascinated but intimidated to realise she wasn't going to be the star of the show, though she spent much of the time dog watching under the pub table.[42]   And then there was Myrtle with our Christmas tree, beside which she appeared to be the largest peke ever seen. The tree was only twelve inches high but of course could have been enormous and she loomed beside it like an elephantine giant peke.

Barbara from New Zealand made her annual trip to see us one year and we decided that Myrtle must be included in our plans. This meant lugging her, our luggage and her buggy into the car, out of the car, onto the train for London, out of the train, down the escalators, onto a different platform, up the escalators, onto another train, out of the train, into a taxi, round the town to the car hire office, out of the taxi, into the hire car eventually, after about seventeen years filling in forms, and finally to our bed and breakfast destination in Dorset.

We had chosen the county of Dorset to visit, influenced to some extent by my interest in T E Lawrence, known as Lawrence of Arabia.

My father had taken me to see Lawrence's home at Clouds Hill when I was seven. Dad had spent most of World War II in the Holy Land and had loved the history and people and had told me such tales of adventure and excitement that it instilled in me a love of those places too.

Lawrence became a legend in his lifetime because of his ability to unite the Arab tribes against the Turks in the First World War. His guerrilla tactics made the stuff of film and many books.

---

[42]Also included was my study of the shape of human ankles, one of my hobbies, along with counting grass blades on walks. Myrtle

Sadly however, his hopes for Arab independence were betrayed when the French and British made a secret treaty to divide the Arab lands between them and Lawrence never recovered from the deception, feeling responsible for misleading his Arab friends.

His exploits were spectacular but he shunned publicity saying: "I've been and am absurdly over-estimated. There are no supermen and I'm quite ordinary, and will say so whatever the artistic results. In that point I'm one of the few people who tell the truth about myself."

More romantically he wrote: "All men dream: but not equally. Those who dream by night in the dusty recesses of their minds wake in the day to find that it was vanity: but the dreamers of the day are dangerous men, for they may act their dreams with open eyes, to make it possible. This I did."

Churchill spoke when Lawrence died, declaring: "We shall not see his like again."

Myrtle shared the room with us. Somehow we had, between us, managed to pack her bed, medicines, blanket, toys and food for a week, goodness knows how, but she settled in quickly home from home.

Each day Barbara and I took Myrtle with us in the back of our hire car, driven bravely by me and navigated even more bravely by Barbara, with Myrtle happy on the back seat, as we went out whatever the weather, on excursions to explore the local places of interest. Myrtle came with us to Corfe Castle in bright sunshine and made the day more fun as we were stopped every few yards by people wanting to stroke her.

Corfe dates back to the time when dinosaurs roamed the area. Nearly all periods of history are in evidence, unequalled in the United Kingdom. On the southern side of the village proof of a civilisation dating from 6,000 BC has been located.

The castle itself in the 17th century, as the English Civil War raged around it, stood firm. The Bankes family supported King Charles I (Cavaliers) against Oliver Cromwell (Roundheads). Lady Bankes defended it bravely through two sieges until she was betrayed by one of her own soldiers.

Myrtle was off on more adventures other days. We drove to Moreton to see Lawrence of Arabia's grave and to have coffee in a Lawrence themed cafe and then the church where Lawrence's funeral had taken place. His funeral was attended by Winston Churchill and other starry dignitaries. Churchill said of Lawrence: "The world looks with some awe upon a man who appears unconcernedly indifferent to home, money, comfort, rank, or even power and fame. Someone strangely enfranchised, untamed, untrammelled by convention, moving independent of the ordinary currents of human action."

On again to see his home, Clouds Hill, which is tiny with hardly any windows. Quite eccentric. After that we drove to the tree where the Tolpuddle Martyrs met and finally to the beautiful Athelhampton House for a walk in the gardens and a cream tea. Myrtle liked cream teas. She also had to have a sticker on her head so that people knew she had paid for her admission to the gardens. She had a wonderful time being stroked and petted and chatted to by the other visitors.

After all that we were reduced to going for a meal in a dog friendly pub. Myrtle was probably hoping she would dig up a dinosaur bone from the Jurassic coast next day where many fossils are found.

She actually proved to be a very clever fossil hunter. Not only did she find a tiny fossil on Kimmeridge Beach[43] but also (so she tried to tell us) the leg of a prehistoric monster which she kindly donated to the fantastic museum in the nearby village. (She was lying). She also wrestled off a large prehistoric sea creature that tried to snatch her off the beach.[44] (More lies - it was in a film in the museum).

What was also very touching was that one of the pretty cottages in the village had a near perfect garden of flowers of every colour, blooming perfumed roses in pinks and yellows and bedding plants to set it all off. When the owner saw Myrtle sitting on his wall and me peering at the display while Barbara was in the museum, he came out and asked if we would like to come in and have a photo taken amongst all the glorious plants. He kindly took several photos and thanked us for our appreciation of his horticultural efforts. What a lovely man!

There was no let up. Next day there was Myrtle again in her buggy like a canine rocket being driven all over Dorset chasing Lawrence of Arabia; going round gardens and stately homes and having a cream tea wherever possible, which was the best bit.

The holiday was a great success. Myrtle was never a problem or a nuisance and seemed to be a star in the sleepy little villages when we clambered out of the car and sat her in her pushchair. People were very taken by it and said their little old dogs stayed at home when they went out and resolved to buy one too. Our host at the guesthouse even let her join us at the breakfast table, something which until meeting Myrtle, he assured us he would never allow any other dog owners to do.

---

[43]I'm sure I'd have found a bigger one if they hadn't been in such a hurry to go to the cafe. Myrtle

[44]Just a small flight of imagination. Wishful thinking. Myrtle

My investment in a pushchair/stroller buggy for her when she was first diagnosed with heart disease at nine years of age, was the best £24 I've ever spent on eBay. It became more and more shabby over the years but still clattered on. It saved so much time and agony waiting for Myrtle to walk when she was tired or me trying to carry what seemed to be a two hundred pound peke.

Lots of people peered into Myrtle's pushchair when we were out, expecting to see a human baby and then leapt backwards in shock at the furry face and bulgy eyes. I would tell them she took after her father.

Then of course there were the local trips out. Not exactly holidays but sometimes a day in Sussex with stunning scenery and a happy little dog seemed like the best holiday in the world. There were bluebell walks with Myrtle and my neighbour Joan, and Autumn days on Ashdown Forest, though no sign of Winnie the Pooh who lived there. Myrtle would decide that being carried was best just as we got to the furthest point of the walk.[45]

Winter squelchy wet walks were often heavy going with a very small dog in a very big forest. Freezing cold wind hit us on some days when she seemed glad to be back indoors. She loved her forest walks but not when she got blown along.

Myrtle was quite keen on trains. She rode on the Tenterden steam railway, seated grandly on a towel on the table so she could see out of the window. When children came to stroke her we spun her round to face them on her towel so they could see her.

---

[45]He he he! Myrtle

One little girl was mesmerised by her and after staring at her intently for quite some time, gently lifted up one of Myrtle's ears and whispered: "Hello Myrtle" very quietly and gave her a soft little kiss. Afterwards Myrtle sat in the garden at the house of the Edwardian actress Ellen Terry and stood looking at the sheep grazing in the field at the end of the garden, rather than admiring the plants.[46]

The Bluebell steam railway which ran from East Grinstead to Sheffield Park was another favourite, chugging through the Sussex scenery into a dreamy, sun filled world from times long ago, when things were mellow and slow and quiet and wheat filled fields stood golden in the summer afternoons.

The skies were blue with big white clouds, the tractor drivers or farm workers waved as we steamed by. I don't suppose they were really waving at Myrtle but we always waved her paw back. She was even given a special ticket marked: "Myrtle the Dog".[47]

Her adventures weren't always far from home but sometimes took a surprising form. One evening my daughter Melissa's father in law had his 80th birthday party in a large hall in the town with wonderful catering, a band and lots of drinks and dancing, so of course Myrtle came too, along with about 200 humans.

Myrtle would stay with my neighbour Joan when I visited my daughter in Ireland. I always felt guilty at deserting her and was restless to get home to retrieve her and hold her warm furry little body in my arms.

---

[46]Sheep are much more interesting than plants. Myrtle

[47]I like to think no other dog had this honour,. Myrtle

Of course in the meantime the neighbour would also get attached to Myrtle and not want to willingly relinquish her back to me without a fight. So for a week after my return she would come round and try to lure Myrtle back to her flat to move in with her, instead of me. In return, I would clutch Myrtle close to me and cover her with kisses and reassurance of my adoration. I always won in the end but Myrtle and my neighbour had a very special bond.

In every church or cathedral I visited without her I would always light a candle for Myrtle. If somewhere out there in the universe there was an omnipotent and caring God, then perhaps he would notice and protect her. Usually I tried to light them by the shrines of St Francis, the saint renowned for his love of, and kindness to, animals.

Perhaps it was part superstition, part belief, part hanging on to anything that might preserve her safely. I don't expect a God out there would be within the scope of our simplistic understanding or react the way we expected him or her to. They may have other agendas than the life of a small black dog. But somehow it helped, so I cannot deny the comfort it brought.

Since she couldn't come with me abroad as she grew older, because of flying being a risk for flat nosed dogs, Myrtle did miss the chance of seeing Buzz Aldrin, the second man to walk on the moon. My cousin and I had flown to Dubai en route to Oman where my elder daughter and family then lived. He happened to be flying on our plane and at Dubai he went past us on one of the electric airport vehicles, smiling and looking very tanned and healthy. I'm sure they would have enjoyed meeting each other. A man who won the space race and a Pekingese who won a prize at the dog show for the dog with the most beautiful legs.

When I was away I always searched for an ornament of a black Pekingese. Though Chinese Fu Dogs were probably the nearest replication of a Pekingese, they didn't seem to resemble the real one I had. From Uzbekistan, to the Middle East, Africa and Australia I searched, but only rarely ornaments of pekes appeared and they were almost always ginger ones. Then in Venice one year in a glass shop in St Marks Square I spotted a black peke. It was tiny but it was a black peke so it came home with me and sits in glory on a shelf, the sole representative of Myrtle as a very small statue.

Paintings however were a bit different. A talented lady in my flat complex painted Myrtle's portrait so well it was indistinguishable from her photograph. Another painting resembles her so much people assume it to be her, though it was actually found in an antique shop in Wales.

A sketch done when she was four hangs in pride of place in my sitting room. Photographs in their thousands, treasured and admired, litter my flat, cupboards, books and computer files. I wanted to remember her completely, every little hair and expression when the time came that we had to part.

Homage was also paid to her by my friend Rosie, whose clever creative talents are quite extraordinary, when she turned up one day with a life sized toy Myrtle that she had made from fur fabric. The resemblance was so strong that the two Myrtles looked like twins, so they were sat together to pose for photos.

Myrtle was furious. "It's an imposter! No-one can replicate me!" She turned her head away from it and ignored it thereafter.[48] I however, and visitors, had quite a few accidental conversations with it in the years to come, thinking it was the real thing.

---

[48]Words cannot describe my indignation. Myrtle

Myrtle made many journeys up to Penrith in Cumbria so that we could be reunited with friends Ann and Alan who we had met in Egypt, and who had returned home to England some time after we did.

When we had left Egypt, Alan, a sergeant major in the army, had been upset that Myrtle was going. When he'd first met her his reaction was: "That's not a dog!" but by the time we decided to return to England months later, he commented that she was the best dog in the world.[49]

Once in London, en route to visit Ann and Alan, we had to negotiate the London Underground. Often kind people carried the case for me as we fought the crowds and little Myrtle looked in danger of being crushed if she wasn't carried. Then it was onto the huge downward escalators into the bowels of the earth, me having to hold Myrtle in my arms, and steady the case and the buggy and keep my balance and step off at the bottom without falling flat. The racket made by the approaching train would have freaked many humans but Myrtle just trotted onto it and either stayed in my arms if I had to stand, or sat in my lap.

She always caused a sensation on the underground trains and was surrounded by people asking questions, stroking her and making the journey a sort of social occasion which Myrtle presided over. Once at Kings Cross station off we got and fought back up the escalators to the main line station. I needed the loo, so Myrtle, the buggy and luggage had to come in the cubicle with me (except Myrtle liked to crawl under the dividing wall to see who was next door which caused both shrieks of shock and amusement.)

---

[49]He was a good judge of character. Myrtle

After that we had to try and find the platform and finally our seat on the train for Penrith, some three hours journey onwards. Mostly Myrtle just slept on my lap, or on the floor, or preferably on the seat next to me with her paws hanging over the edge. Sometimes she stood on her hind legs and watched the world whizzing by through the window. Frequently passers-by stopped to talk to her. Occasionally railway employees asked me to put her on the floor but I sneaked her back onto the seat, sitting on and covered by my coat when they had gone.

Finally, we would stagger off the train at Penrith and meet up with Ann and Alan. We usually stayed in their home and from there travelled off to see Gretna Green in Scotland, Lake Windermere for a boat ride, and Hadrian's Wall in Northumberland. Myrtle sat with me in the back of their car and had a wonderful time exploring new territory, including their lovely garden.

One year when Barbara was over from New Zealand we stayed in a bed and breakfast place in Penrith and hired a car. We stopped to buy traditional gingerbread in Grasmere and walked round Keswick and greeted all the other dogs doing the same thing.

Myrtle was included in everything we did, and came wherever we went.

The Lake District scenery was stunning with mountains and winding roads reflected in the lakes. In summer it was a tourist paradise but a different world in winter when thick snow on the mountain tops and icy roads meant danger. The temperature was often below freezing and the light was strange and thin, turning the snow topped peaks pink just before darkness fell.

After the holidays ended, of course we'd have to do the whole journey back to Sussex again, which was if anything, more of a nightmare, as the Penrith to London train was always crowded. Myrtle would progress along different laps until she found someone who seemed more comfortable than I evidently was.

Once I fell asleep on the train and was awoken by a lady holding Myrtle by her lead and explaining that she had wandered off up the corridor into the next carriage and had been royally entertained by all the passengers[50] until someone suggested she might have an owner and they had set out to find me. Myrtle of course just walked straight back to where I was.

They were happy times.

---

[50]Understandably I made their journey enjoyable. Myrtle

Brighton sweet shop

Grave of Lawrence of Arabia

Ticket for the Bluebell Railway

The Bluebell Railway ticket

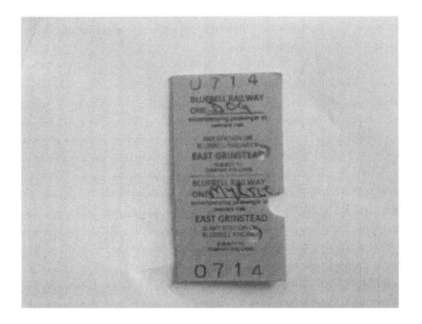

Boarding the boat in the English Lake District

Ready to appear on Trinny & Susannah

At Scotney Castle

Sir Winston Churchill, Westerham

Cafe in Dorset

Waiting for a drink in a pub

Roman Hadrian's Wall

Borde Hill Gardens

Myrtle's Poem

From the pyramids of Egypt to the bustling old bazaars
I have seen the ships on Suez and the desert under stars
I have crossed the Sinai mountains and met camels on the road
The Red Sea held no fear for me nor heat or mosquitoes.
I sheltered under palm trees and tossed my head at flies.
I learned to love the sights and sounds beneath Arabian skies.
I have travelled far by aeroplane and bus and boat and train
And walked on sand that burned my paws, knew sun and wind
and rain.
I've watched the gentle greying skies above my Sussex home
And run down forest paths and ways where deer and badgers
roam.
As I grew ill my memories were kindness, care and fun
And I shall leave in loving arms when my sweet life is done.

Chapter 8

Myrtle's Daily Life

No one can really sum up the personality of a dog that isn't their own because you need to be with it constantly to get the true measure of its quirks and habits. Only by recounting incidents can the true spirit of Myrtle shine through. There were so many but these next are the ones that show her impact most.

My favourite memory of Myrtle was when I took her to visit Hadrian's Wall, built by the Romans to keep out the northern tribes. Right in the northern outreaches of England in Northumberland, this ancient wall still stands in wild and rolling barren country with views north towards Scotland and anyone advancing. Again, as in parts of Ashdown Forest, there was a sense of personalities, invisible but watching, not necessary malign but perhaps indignant or bewildered by our presence.

After Myrtle had sat on the wall surveying the view, we rested at a table outside. Nearby sat an Indian lady in a colourful silk sari, with her daughter. After a few moments the daughter approached me and said: "I've been trying to describe your dog to my mother, who is blind. Would you mind if she stroked her?"

I put Myrtle in the older lady's lap and she held her close, feeling her ears and face and her paws, tail and legs and cuddling and stroking her. All the time the older lady said again and again: "She's beautiful!" And tears rolled down her cheeks. The daughter kept thanking me and was crying too.

The experience made a profound impact on me and was instrumental in prolonging Myrtle's life but that is a story for a future chapter.

The emotions that were felt seeing the effect Myrtle had on the Indian lady, made me recall my association with the Mary Rose, Henry VIII's flagship at the time it was raised from the seabed in 1982.

As I'd fund raised for the Mary Rose, one of the divers said he'd give some souvenirs for my kids, as he had relatives somewhere in Sussex. My children had been dressed as Henry VIII and two of the wives and had raised nearly £500 walking up and down the seafront at Southsea the day the Mary Rose was due to be raised. I made the costumes out of old curtains and broken costume jewellery.

In the event we missed the ship being raised as the authorities postponed the raising until the following day.

When the news came through that it had been postponed, we were standing by a man on a bench with his head in his hands and he looked up and said: " I've been fascinated by the Mary Rose since I was a kid and always vowed if they raised it I'd be there. I've come down from Liverpool to see it today but I have to go back tonight as I've been unemployed for four years and I've got a job interview tomorrow. I'm just too disappointed for words but seeing you and your lovely children has made the trip worthwhile. You can have all the money in my wallet," and he emptied what little he had into our tin.

The Hadrian's Wall incident with Myrtle and the Portsmouth one so many years before with my children, made me realise how many lonely people there are out there who can be uplifted by even a small light in the darkness of their days.

Some years ago I came out of the doctor's to to find a man peering through my car window. "Is that Myrtle in there?" he asked. I said it was.

"Please can you send me some photos of her so I can show my mother?" he asked. Taken aback, I was stuttering and mystified and so he explained:

"My mother has a pug called Wilbur and he used to stay with a lady who looked after mostly big dogs. Wilbur used to get badly bullied. Then one day we went to collect him and all the big dogs were cowering in a corner of the garden and Wilbur was playing with Myrtle on the lawn. She'd come to stay for the day and had protected Wilbur and chased off five or six of the large dogs. NO ONE messes with Myrtle," he said and continued: "We saw her once in the town afterwards and wanted to stop to talk to her but we couldn't find anywhere to park." (I assume he meant she was with me).

So I sent him photos of Myrtle, and Wilbur sent some back of himself to her. Pekingese are such brave little dogs. It always amuses me to imagine her driving off the baddies.[51]

Myrtle was always well looked after when I sent her to stay with the lady who also had Wilbur. She had been my neighbour some forty years previously. On occasion my kind boss's wife would have her instead on their farm where she was a nuisance pursuing chicken and rushing off in all directions.

Myrtle made a new conquest in the shape of the carer who was looking after the old lady Audrey, who lived opposite me at our flat in the village. She kept knocking and coming in to see Myrtle (not me you may notice).

On 12 December 2015 Myrtle acted in an extraordinary way which resulted in the rescue of Audrey who had fallen in her flat and was unable to get up.

---

[51]Just one look was enough. Myrtle

Had Myrtle not drawn attention to the situation, Audrey could have lain there for many more hours without food or water before anyone called round, or even died due to the cold.

That morning I had been shopping and finally got home about 2pm. I was unwell and fell asleep on the sofa, waking up when it was dark.

Myrtle ran into the hall as soon as I put the light on, and was scrabbling and snuffling at my front door. I thought she needed the loo, so dragged myself up and got ready to go down the road. As soon as I opened the door, she flung herself at Audrey's door opposite, clawing and scratching at it. I dragged her away and down the road. She put her brakes on and turned and heaved me back towards the flats.

When we were inside, Myrtle flung herself back at Audrey's door with even more ferocious determination. I was cross with her in case she disturbed Audrey and again tried to pull her back indoors.

She was having none of it. Despite being very small and weighing about 11 pounds, she appeared to have the ability to magically increase her weight to what seemed to be about 14 stone, and nothing I could do was going to move her from Audrey's door, despite my pulling and cajoling.

She became so frantic that I finally approached the door myself.[52] I am quite deaf and had to listen hard but thought I could hear a faint cry for help. Audrey had fallen hours before and couldn't get up, frightened and alone in the dark.

---

[52]Short of bulldozing down the door I did all I could. Myrtle

While Myrtle continued worrying and whining at the door, I called through the letterbox to say I was getting help. Abandoning Myrtle at her position, I ran and pulled the emergency cord in my own flat to alert Lifeline but with no response.

I ran and knocked for another resident, who was friendly with Audrey. Neither of us could get inside but from outside through the window we could see her on the floor in the bedroom doorway. I went back to my flat and pulled the cord again and this time got an answer and was told Lifeline would notify someone at once.

Finally the key-holder arrived and was able to access the flat. She and another neighbour picked up Audrey and helped her to the sofa to give her some water. Everyone petted and praised Myrtle for being a heroine and said she should be on TV.

Myrtle and I were by now cold from standing outside in the rain and I was feeling shaken and affected by it all. We felt we could do no more and so went home. Myrtle once again stopped by the lady's door as if she was checking things were OK now.[53]

Some days later Myrtle and I called round and all seemed well. One of her friends stopped us in the street to thank us with a big hug.

Myrtle's actions that night raised her profile at the flats and she was fussed and praised whenever she appeared. The residents felt she was an asset rather than a possible pest.

---

[53]If you want something done properly, do it yourself. Myrtle

As a result of the local newspaper spotting the story on Facebook, Myrtle was awarded a PDSA Commendation (Peoples Dispensary for Sick Animals) who contacted me after reading about her actions. They wanted to award her a commendation for bravery which had at that time only been granted to 66 animals since its inauguration in 2001.

It was the Christmas party at the flats in mid December after we moved to the village, so Myrtle came along to bring cheer to the proceedings. Not that the expressions on the guests' faces looked cheerful but she was much fussed over. She wore her golden ringlets for the occasion which were a Christmas parcel decoration of spiralled golden metallic ribbon.

Earlier when I was at the hairdresser, someone knocked over a dish of hair dye which splashed onto her fur so she had one blonde streak, which I assured her would make her very fashionable and would cost a fortune normally. Myrtle was the Christmas Fairy for the old people's party. She ate most of their food.[54]

I heard from Hat Trick Productions (RDF TV) the following year, saying they would like Myrtle to appear on a TV programme about dogs, as a result of the PDSA award given for alerting her to Audrey's fall. They asked lots of questions about Myrtle and for photos of her. They made the Father Ted series in the 1990s, amongst other things which was a bit of a surprise.

Their general idea was that most awards went to large, brave, strong dogs like German Shepherds or Retrievers and so Myrtle, tiny little thing that she was, could make the programme a bit different.

---

[54] I suppose I could have sung to them instead. Myrtle

The programme was in its very early stages. Autographs would have been by paw print on request of course, but sadly I felt unable to involve Audrey in this proposed enterprise due to her age and frailty, and without her being interviewed, Hat Trick Productions felt Myrtle wouldn't tell the story very well on her own. So it never came to anything.

For years I have been very hard of hearing. Deafness is a socially isolating condition. It makes an animal an even more valuable companion because you don't have to listen to its answer when you speak. I gave in in the end and ordered hearing aids which finally arrived. I put them in and shortly afterwards realised Myrtle was making odd breathing noises as if she was going to explode. I rushed her to my neighbour who said she always made snorting noises and spluttering sounds and didn't sound any different from usual. Then I was aware of the clock ticking, like a hammer.

As soon as I removed the hearing aids Myrtle sounded normal again and the world seemed peaceful. What a lot I had been missing but calm and quiet was lost when I wore them. When I walked, my footsteps sounded like Jack the Giant Killer, birds shouted from the trees and people seemed to speak through megaphones.

It was even more embarrassing when I was at a lunch in Ireland with the family and friends, and asked my granddaughter what she had chosen from the menu. "Teabags," she announced with confidence. I tried for a few seconds to process this information. "What did you say?" I ventured. "TEABAGS!" she bellowed, obviously thinking my brain had shrivelled and died. "Oh!" I said knowledgeably, assuming it must be some Irish delicacy. It turned out to be Sea Bass.

Then on the way home in the car I mentioned how lovely the perfume was in the air freshener and asked my daughter what it was called. "Fresh bottom," she replied. "Really?" I said, astounded, "What an extraordinary name for an air freshener!" After ten more minutes of screeching and incredulity she managed to transmit to me that she had been saying: "Fresh cotton".

So the hearing aids had to be used from then on.

During the summer I had to take an old chair to our local dump and Myrtle came for the ride. When we arrived, five men, who were helpers at the dump, clustered around the car, which was slightly scary as they looked like the sort you'd avoid on a dark night. One of them spoke as I tried to get the chair out and asked what sort of dog Myrtle was.

Soon we were surrounded with his workmates all wanting to stroke her and making cooing noises at her and generally turning into melted jellies at her little face. They were totally smitten with her. That would teach me not to judge books by their covers.

Some years before I had answered the door to a young man selling tea towels and dusters from a large zipper bag. I asked why he was doing such a job and he explained that he'd been in a young offenders' unit for breaking and entering property to steal but was now out and keen to set his life right. I felt a surge of emotion at the uphill struggle he had before him and gave a few kind but sensible words to try and keep him on the straight and narrow.

At this point the front door slammed behind me and I was locked out.

"Don't worry," said my newly reformed friend, "I'll get inside for you!" and with that he climbed onto the porch roof, reached through the open upstairs fanlight, undid the big window, climbed inside and ran down the stairs and opened the front door to me, smiling broadly that he'd been able to put his skills to use.

Myrtle who had watched the proceedings from indoors had a slightly baffled expression at all this activity.[55]

Myrtle liked football on television but got annoyed that she couldn't get inside and join in. She was very enthusiastic about watching the World Cup. She didn't like her patriotic paper hat though. When the players ran off the screen she peered round the side of the television waiting to catch them. I think she thought they lived in the storage unit at the side of it.

For some reason she also really enjoyed a Western, preferably starring John Wayne. She would be glued to the film and seemed to be following the story. She enjoyed the saloon fights best.[56]

She once spent the entire evening riveted to the film Jurassic World, barking at the monsters and standing on her back legs to get at them. In some of her wilder moments, she was lunging at the television and shouting threats at the dinosaurs.

---

[55]Only Daphne could happily agree for a young offender break into her house. Myrtle

[56]John Wayne is ace! Myrtle

Her favourite Disney film was 101 Dalmatians. She was such a tele addict. She would recognise Paul O'Grady's face and start barking because she knew there would be some dogs appearing if he was on TV doing his programme on Battersea Dogs Home.

In an episode of Midsomer Murders there was a man who appeared at the beginning with a dog. This caused her to hurl herself at the screen barking wildly. By the end of the two hour episode she was rushing to the television when the man was on, even without the dog. She had recognised his face and associated him with his dog, even when it didn't appear.

Myrtle appeared on television very briefly. My daughter and I were asked to fill in when two ladies due to appear on the television show "Trinny and Susannah" were ill with flu.

Myrtle and my daughter's dog were to come with us. The idea was to contrast ladies with huge dogs and the way they may choose to dress, with those who had little dogs and tended to go for glamour. I don't think this is necessarily a correct assumption but it formed the basis for the show.

Six ladies with big dogs and six with small. Then we had to turn up in our own choice of clothing and Trinny and Susannah would put us right on what we should be wearing. We were taken to the studios in London by limo with Myrtle peering grandly from the window.[57]

After the filming we returned home to Gatwick and were joined on the train by the charming Paul Costello, the Irish fashion designer, who chatted to us the whole way home. Myrtle rather liked mixing with the world of fame and entertainment. She was disappointed to have ended up mostly on the cutting room floor bar a few seconds clip.

---

[57]This is my preferred means of transport. Myrtle

After I returned from hospital following a shoulder replacement, I noticed Myrtle looked at me blankly. Then I had a terrible thought. The reason was that since the operation I hadn't put any makeup on! She didn't recognise me and wondered who on earth had taken up residence in her home! When I made an effort after this and put on the usual makeup she came to me at once.

No wonder she looked bewildered but more horribly my make up must transform me into someone else!

Myrtle loved visitors as long as the idea was that they'd come to visit her, not me. When my friend Wendy used a cushion on her lap to balance the iPad to look up something while she was here, Myrtle wanted to sit on the cushion. Thus Wendy was unable to see or use the iPad. Myrtle had never sat on a cushion before in her life.

Myrtle knew the names of all of my friends. When the doorbell rang at the flat we moved to when she grew older, her ears would prick up and she would rush to the front door. I would open it and say: "Go and see Nick, or Melissa, or Rosie and Hugh, or Wendy, or Julie," or whoever it was and she would stand poised like a pointer waiting for the visitor to appear round the corner at the end of the passage leading to the front door.

Then galvanised instantly into a gallop she would fly up the passage, ears flying, short little legs hardly making contact with the carpet, into the arms and kind words of whoever was coming to see us.

Sometimes was only the postman and she came dismally back looking cheated, but when it was a friend or family member she leapt around accompanying them down to my flat. As far as her figure allowed she would do somersaults and handstands to show what a happy healthy little creature she was, even if three minutes before they rang the bell she appeared to be about to expire.

In her entire life she never knew anything but love, kindness, affection and care. Many human children have less. On the few borderline occasions where bad temper or malice was directed towards her it marked the end of my relationship with the people concerned. One boyfriend knocked her off the sofa as she sat beside me because he was angry about something I'd said. Goodbye boyfriend.

She would sit and listen to my conversations with friends, looking from one to the other as if she perfectly understood what we were saying and was digesting all the information. She seemed not to realise she was a dog at all but some family member who had inadvertently turned out looking a bit different from the rest of us.

As the years passed Myrtle started to develop delusions of grandeur. When she heard the name Mrs Merkel, the German chancellor on the news, she would rush to the television thinking the announcer was saying Mrs Myrtle. She also was flattered by the commentator at all the Royal weddings on television persistently referring to myrtle in the bouquets. She would run to the screen whenever the commentator mentioned it, obviously delighted to have been included in the celebrations.[58]

---

[58] I can't understand why Prince Harry chose Meghan instead of me. Myrtle

As a pet she was as near to being perfect as I could wish for. But she did have a few quirks. She would happily burst out through the cat flap into the garden at the cottage but would doggedly refuse to come back in by the same means.

She would sit outside peering through the glass Perspex swing door, whatever the weather, rain, hail, sleet, or snow, looking as pathetic as she could muster until I physically opened the back door and allowed her to make an entrance. She would sleep absolutely centrally on my bed leaving me to cling onto the edge for fear of falling out.

Unusually for a small dog she rarely barked. She would alert me to someone knocking at the door or shout abuse at dogs on television but otherwise apart from grunting and snorting she didn't make a racket or yap. She also had an unusually strong affection for cats and kittens and never showed any aggression towards them.

If I used the vacuum cleaner, which she considered to be a malformed bird of ill omen wanting to curtail her existence on planet earth, she would flee, rolling the whites of her eyes and tucking her tail under her, in case the cleaner lunged at her and ate her.

I didn't have a good relationship with the vacuum cleaner either. For a start it was like pushing a World War II tank and sucked up everything in its path from shoes to rugs, so a large portion of my time was taken dismantling it to retrieve valuables from its stomach.

Only once did I ever see it cowed. I'd discovered that the skirting board in a corner had a layer of dust along it that looked like a black snake.

Assuming it actually was unlikely to be one, I ran my finger along and produced a large lump of dust and fluff. As I pushed the Hoover towards it I could have sworn it jerked back in fear and horror at the size of it. I never was much one for housework.

Myrtle also developed an utter loathing for the main trustee's little terrier at the cottage when we lived there, and would throw herself at the fence barking like a canine banshee, shrieking abuse at it and trying to wedge her nose under the fence in the hope it would voluntarily offer itself to be bitten.

No doubt animals do absorb traits of their owners[59]. Her attitude to Seamus who lived on the other side of our cottage, was adoration, acceptance and affection.

On the plus side, she was cuddly and sweet natured, travelled happily in the car, didn't cost much to feed and played happily with her toys. She would push her little face up to mine and incline her head to lean against my chest, staring up at my face with her big saucer like eyes with their deep and unfathomable expression.

The bond I had with her was unlike anything I had every experienced before with an animal. It felt as if we were matched down to last molecule. I never had cause to reprimand her or be angry. Her trust in me extended to allowing me to trim the fur around her eyes without any objection, as she lay still with eyes open while I did it. She loved to sit on my lap and watch television of an evening. She also loved lions and if I put on a DVD of Christian the Lion who had been bought in Harrods and then released into the wild in Kenya, she would come in from the kitchen at a gallop as soon as the church bells sounded at the start of the film.

---

[59]How disturbing. Myrtle

If I was asked to say in just one sentence what Myrtle was and what she meant to me, the first word that I would speak would be "Joy". Then her energy, her affection, her beauty, her humour, her completely confident take on the world and her total appreciation and engagement with life.

I had hoped she would outlive Pookie's age of thirteen years and four months.

I imagined she would live to be at least fifteen, by which time I'd be in my mid seventies and ready to move out of the cold and damp cottage and away from the isolation of the forest. In the end we moved to a warm flat in our local village of Forest Row, when she was ten, when both her heart and my bones had started to give out.

Tenterden Light Railway Station

I want to be a wallaby!

My three children in their Tudor costumes

Meeting a Newfoundland

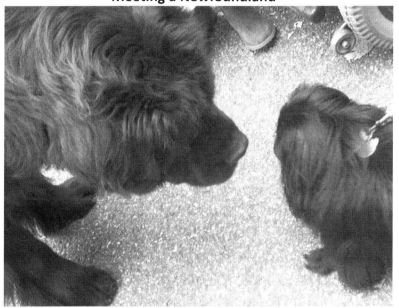

On the train

Church Visit in Kent

SAT
5 °C
Clear

🏠 News   Sport   What's On   Jobs   Property   Cars   Directory   Notices   Offers

Persistent dog helps to save pensioner's life after fall

By **East Grinstead Courier** | Posted: April 24, 2016   By Wojciech Zdrojkowski

VIEW GALLERY

Just checking after the fall

The PDSA Award

Meeting friends

More friends

Saying hello to strangers

Hello to a friend from online

Forest rest

Hever Castle, Kent

Up a Tree in Sheffield Park Gardens

Waiting in a cafe

Chapter 9

And Then the Blow Fell

Myrtle's meeting with the Indian lady at Hadrian's wall, mentioned in the previous chapter, had made a profound impact on me and made me realise the extraordinary magic that emanated from Myrtle and her potential to change things for the better for people around her.

I decided as a result, to enrol Myrtle to visit hospitals and hospices to comfort sick and dying people. She had to have up to date injections and we returned for the booster injections two weeks later.

It was then that I was told Myrtle was very ill with heart failure and would not live for much longer. So she never got to fulfil my dream of helping sick people but thanks to her vet and the love she received from everyone around her and from all over the world through her photos on the Internet, she had so many further years of life.

Again and again in the future she was to defy the vet's predictions and came back from the edge, after looking over the precipice into death.

The love of so many who knew her, and those who did not but followed her online from all over the world, seemed to draw on a force that pulled her back time and again.[60]

No one knew or guessed that her diagnosis of imminent heart failure would bring my life and nerves crashing or that there on after I expected every day to be her last.

---

[60]Hello all peke friends worldwide. I love you all! Myrtle

Some days she seemed quiet and introspective, as if she knew about her bad heart condition even before I did, but at other times she would gain huge energy and stamina and race around like a thing demented.

I loved her so much and it was torture for me to watch and wonder. I tried not to cosset her too much. I wanted her life to be good and carefree and happy and unrestricted, even if short, not boring and closed with long protracted suffering.

It was therefore, at the age of nine, on that routine visit to her vet, that Myrtle was diagnosed as seriously ill, and the news shocked me to the core. I hadn't the slightest notion that this was the case. I'd wondered if she was maybe slightly off colour but never that she was likely to be snatched from me at such a young age. The vet quoted a figure approaching £3,000 to test her for the heart condition he suspected but that was so far beyond my budget that I picked her up and walked out.

I drove back to our village and enlisted with Alex the vet there, without telling him what had been told to me half an hour before. After a thorough examination, he said almost word for word exactly the same thing, whereupon I disintegrated. He was a compassionate and caring young man. Apparently he'd wanted to save all the animals in the world from the age of two. He bypassed all the tests and worked on a best guess basis with tablets instead, from that moment onwards.

When the news was confirmed to me I physically shook. Feelings swept over me which were familiar but which I couldn't identify. It took me several days to understand what those feelings meant and when I had felt them before. It was like losing a human child and was the same desperate hopelessness that I had endured when I was told so many decades before that my human baby couldn't live with his congenital heart condition. He had died a week later.

Myrtle had thus lived with CHD, mitral valve failure and an enlarged heart since she was nine.

She was thirteen in March 2019. Without medicine I would have lost her long before. She eventually had Vetmedin, Fortekor and Viagra daily. She had never had an ECG or scan because of the cost. I also switched her to a home cooked diet and gave her Q10 tablets but they were huge like submarines and she often spat them out.

Allegedly sildenafil, otherwise known as Viagra, was first discovered for the treatment of heart disease in dogs and then as a side effect its assistance with impotence was revealed. The principle was similar. It opens up the blood vessels. In Myrtle's case to her heart.

Until a wise lady on one of the online peke groups suggested it[61], I like most people, hadn't heard of the use of Viagra for dogs with bad hearts. I mentioned it to the vet when I first was told about it but Alex had said it was too expensive at £20 a tablet.

The problem was knowing when to relax and when to jump and land in the vet's surgery. She could go from being a circus performer to death's door in five minutes flat.

When she was ill, it felt as if the love, prayers and people's tears from all over the world came to comfort me and their healing power seemed to make her well time and again. Whatever one says about the Internet, the power of uniting people in a common good is nothing short of miraculous.[62]

---

[61]You know who you are and I owe my life to your advice xxx Myrtle

[62]Hear hear! Myrtle

Myrtle in 2019 had been with me for twelve years of her thirteen, bearing in mind she had come to live with me when she was almost one. She had not only serious heart problems but her sight wasn't good. She was sweet and didn't bite or snap.

My priority was for her happiness, not for what would make me happy for the future. Despite being tempted numerous times by rescues or peke pups, I decided to see her life out in the way she'd always known it - being totally in charge of me, with me being a sort of on call servant for love, food, outings etc. And more to the point on a one to one basis with me and no other dog in competition.[63]

She was the reason I bothered to go for a walk, or sometimes even go out of the flat, or get up on bad mornings. She was my friend, child, companion, confidant, teddy bear and part of my daily life. I wanted her life to be happy from start to finish and if she was ever in pain or too ill to cope, then I must suffer the pain of her loss if it meant stopping the pain in her.

Myrtle's vet now greeted her with: "Hello Myrtle. How come you're still here? You should be dead!" and then covered her with kisses and talked to her in a high silly voice. Fortunately I knew he was joking and he was very kind.[64]

Despite multiple prognoses of imminent departure, Myrtle trotted on having a wonderful time. Medically she was a disaster but she hadn't the slightest interest in medical predictions - she just liked being Myrtle. I do put down her survival to Viagra and home cooking and lots of outings and very very close watching for any adverse signs. She had to be on borrowed time but at this rate she would outlive me.

---

[63]One of me is enough for anyone. Myrtle

[64]Well I didn't think it was funny! Myrtle

She was so precious to me

One of the sadnesses of having a dog or cat is that their life expectancy is not equal to ours so there must be, by the natural rule of things, many sad goodbyes over our own human lifetimes.

Myrtle's vet must have thought I was a neurotic nutter who ran in crying whenever Myrtle sneezed. However despite his working on more or less palliative care with her and reducing costs to absolute basic, his attitude seemed to suit her health. She loathed him.

Anxiety is a horrible thing. It seeps into every part of your being, every minute of your day. It wakes you at night, it knocks on the door of your heart in dreams and slaps you in the face in the morning. It gnaws at you when you are out and supposedly enjoying yourself with friends. It sits in your shoulder when you are alone. It forces you to check not once or twice but every few hours in every twenty four that your beloved pet is still breathing.

Every time I had been out without Myrtle, I had to stop and take a breath before I put my key in the front door, and instantly called her name as I went in. For a few moments there would be nothing and the thoughts of her being dead would strangle my mind. Then a little furry black face would peer around the corner at me, her tail would wag and I'd sweep her into my arms and cover her with kisses and often with tears.

Even with severe heart problems she could still shoot off if it suited her, instead of her usual drifting about sniffing grass blades. It's amazing the speed they can reach when you're chasing them. I should have carried a huge butterfly net around with me to zap her if she got away, and before she launched off like a greyhound from a trap you could almost hear her gathering up her engine for an escape.[65]

---

[65] I should never be underestimated. Myrtle

I took her to the little dog show at the vet's, in her pushchair because of the heat but she seemed to enjoy it and was as usual much admired. Alex the vet rushed up and listened to her heart and said the beat was stronger and the fluid on her lungs was less now that the medication was higher but he didn't want to repeat the diuretics if her lungs seemed clear. Apparently overuse can damage the kidneys. I could see she wasn't really well but still she veered towards being so much better than earlier in the week when every moment I thought I was going to lose her. And so we went on.

It was this roller coaster of fear, hope, certain knowledge and insane optimism that racked me for all those years when she was ill. I could only deal with it by keeping myself occupied by taking her out and giving her a life which gave her joy, company, fun, attention and memories for us both.[66]

When she was first diagnosed, she was given just one year to live. Two months later it was said to be only two weeks, maybe even just hours. She was still enjoying her life and eating well but didn't ever have proprietary dog food any more. I cooked and fed her better than I fed myself. She would have Aberdeen Angus minced beef with sweet potato, broccoli, spinach, carrot, celery, brown rice, spelt, pearl barley, lentils, tomato, parsnip and pumpkin seeds all mixed into a stew for lunch and then poached salmon or white fish pieces from the fish and chip shop for her dinner. It was made bulk and portions frozen and didn't cost more than some of the tinned stuff. I had beans on toast.

She didn't like taking her tablets though. She rejected them hidden in sardines, breast of chicken, raw minced steak, cheese, butter, sausage, dog food and just being stuffed down her throat. She managed to spit one out one morning and it was found hanging in one of her ears.

---

[66]And indeed you did. Myrtle

In the end my neighbour cracked it by soaking a biscuit in tea and hiding a tablet in bits of it. Myrtle, who considered anything humans ate should have been first offered to her, was delighted to be included in the tea and biscuit scenario and would gobble it up.

Often Myrtle, the dog who was about to depart this life any moment, would spring up and start killing her toy pig.[67]

As the years progressed that she survived, the toll that her health scare had taken on me started to affect my health too. I didn't slept and spent hours crying. I honestly think she invented injuries and diseases to entertain me in dull moments.

Sometimes she would sit and stare at me as if to try and jolly me out of my gloom by getting me to take her out in the car: "I'm dreaming of hang gliding or maybe bungee jumping," she seemed to be saying. So off we would go and another day with us together was ticked off.

The vet told me that she should never be allowed to jump off chairs or the bed because of her bad arthritic spine so Myrtle had steps bought at great expense so she could go up and down, on and off furniture. She ignored them totally, greeting any attempt to help her up and down them with an expression of horror akin to being enticed off a high cliff to fall onto rocks. I threw them away in the end. Other animals are of a more grateful nature.

I considered myself blessed with a compassionate and clever vet and a dog with a huge desire to live life to the full. And yet..... there were some who knew us who sneered that she was still going strong.

---

[67]Someone had to do it. Myrtle

Friends saw my own health deteriorate with the strain, and migraines and insomnia made my life miserable. I knew sooner or later I would lose her before her deserved lifespan. It was so painful to me. It was a lonely road to travel.[68]

Three years almost to the day since her first diagnosis of heart problems, Myrtle had a heart attack. She got out of her bed first thing in the morning and walked towards her second bed in the sitting room, staggered sideways, fell onto her side with a scream and then lay still.

I found myself at the vet. Myrtle lay in front of me on his operating table. I don't remember phoning him or driving down there or going through his door. It was a Wednesday and he showed me out of his surgery with the words: "Whatever her death may be it will be horrible unless you end things very soon. If she has another heart attack she will have terrible fear and pain. If her lungs fill, she will drown in her own body fluids. Call me on Friday and I will come and put her to sleep at your flat. It is the kindest thing."

I carried her inert little body home, kissing and holding her close to me. That night as the vet had instructed, I gave her half a Viagra tablet morning and evening. By the Friday she was practising ballet round the room and somersaulting about with her toys. Myrtle had lived to fight another day. At exactly the time of her heart attack the price of Viagra had suddenly dropped and so Alex prescribed it. It worked.

---

[68]But I'll always be with you somehow. Myrtle

Myrtle hated Alex the vet and squeaked and shook with terror as we waited to see him, though once she was in his consulting room she became less of a jelly. On one occasion she seemed suddenly to develop dandruff. Strange foam was spread all over her by Alex to soften her skin, so she looked like one of those brushes in a car wash. Her weight was always steady 5.4 kilos, roughly twelve pounds.

Alex would say that he thought he would never be rid of us. We would still be his patients in 2030 but he was really genuinely delighted to see her so well. Myrtle left the surgery every time at 150 miles an hour and fled to the car to escape his clutches. She was thrilled to be leaving him.

She had her long overdue heart check-up in late July of that year.
Alex had of course wanted to see her five weeks before with a view to putting her to sleep but thanks to Viagra she had been pretty well since and only because it was soon a bank holiday was I taking her back that day. Alex held her up and kissed her "You love proving me wrong," he said to her. She was truly the Duracell bunny of the dog world.

Watching a loved one slide deeper into ill health is like living in a nightmare where you can hear the hooves of a galloping horse behind you, getting nearer and nearer and louder and louder but don't know when it's going to get you. I'd been grieving in advance all this time and it made me terrified of her illness instead of adjusting to it. I enjoyed and was grateful for every moment with her and she had lots of outings and adventures and enjoyed her life, but in the dark of the night I felt such fear of losing her.

Long ago when my son Nick was about six he had a little golden hamster called Superman. When Superman was about two he seemed to develop a sort of chest infection and sounded as if he was wheezing. Nick spent hours sobbing and holding Superman, until my then husband took the hamster to the vet and brought him home again, having had an injection to help the chest infection heal. Nick continued to cry and lurk about Superman's cage, stroking him and soaking him with his tears.

Next day, after Nick had gone to school I found Superman dead. I anguished all day about how I was going to break the news to Nick and how to deal with his reaction. I warned his sisters that we would need to have a State Funeral in the garden with hymns, appropriate prayers, flowers, a small handmade cross to mark the grave and to be especially kind to Nick in his grief.

Finally Nick returned from school and I broke the news to him, "And we're going to have a lovely funeral in the garden for Superman!" I finished up triumphantly.

"OK can I watch Blue Peter?" said Nick. (This was a kids' television programme in those days).

"Don't you want to come to Superman's funeral?" I asked, bewildered.

"No", said Nick, "I was only upset because I thought he was ill and suffering. Now he's dead it's OK, because he isn't in pain. I hated seeing him sick and I didn't know how to help him," and with that he turned and watched his television programme, while his sisters and I conducted the funeral without him, and probably tortured the neighbours with our rendering of "All Things Bright and Beautiful".

I have often thought since of Nick's reaction to his hamster's illness and subsequent death and thought that perhaps it does, to some extent, mirror what I was going through with Myrtle all those years, terrified she might be feeling ill or her wanting to ask me to help her and me not understanding.

Perhaps then when her end came, I would feel a sense of release for her and for myself from all the worrying and vet visits. That may have been so but it would be mixed with loss, loneliness, with grief, emptiness and a sense of finality too.

So how do I explain this pain. This all consuming obsession with this tiny little furry creature that shared my life? Was this neurosis rooted back in the past when I had known the loss of both my father and son within eighteen months so that fear of loss became constant from then on?

Was it my childhood, being an only child, my aloneness, my lack of love as an adult, my feeling of distance, of rejection, of no one knowing or caring about the Me in me? Or was it perhaps that I had been given this wonderful gift of a small animal that lightened every day and mood, and made me smile and feel a sense of belonging and purpose? Maybe it was all those things combined.

A few days after the next vet visit, a man came to mend my broken shower. Myrtle went leaping up to him and brought him all her teddies. He couldn't believe it was the same sick dog he had seen a month before when he came to fix my door. He made a big fuss of her and was so delighted to see her on top form.

Unfortunately, or maybe fortunately, all the crises in the last three years had genuinely been life threatening and dangerous and she had been scooped back by Alex's care and the magic of modern drugs. Just because she had survived didn't mean she wasn't ill or that these emergencies weren't real, neither did it mean that sooner or later one such emergency wouldn't result in her death.

The shower mending man went off smiling to tell his wife that to his surprise Myrtle was still with me, large as life and looking good.

I think it's a peke worldwide conspiracy to get attention and remind us of their worth while taking every penny we have in vet fees.[69] Within four seconds of my paying the bill Myrtle would burst into song and do acrobatic tricks.

Myrtle and I drove up to the forest a few evenings later as the sun was sinking and the temperature cooling slightly. She wasn't up to walking far. Her legs had become very wobbly in the last two days and she kept gagging and scratching her sides. I didn't know if this was a sign of deterioration or just the hot weather.

We sat on a wooden bench together side by side in silence and just looked at the view for a long while. She sat right up close to me as if she was reassuring me that she was a part of me and that we were best buddies. I carried her back to the car. I so wished the hot weather would break and give her a chance.

---

[69]Well we do like to keep you on your toes. Myrtle

Next morning, Myrtle the famous everlasting dog woke up and was perfectly normal.[70] Quite miraculous. If you had seen her the day before you would have doubted she would make it overnight. The vet phoned and said to put salmon oil on her food, give her something that sounded like lipid green mussels from the health shop (he had a heavy Spanish accent) and also that the surgery did offer acupuncture if she needed it.

A few days later and back yet again to the vet. Because Myrtle was now practising ballet pirouettes and generally showing the energy and exuberance of a stabled carthorse suddenly let out to grass, it was hard for the vet who saw her (as Alex was now away on holiday), to interpret the frightening sequence of events of the previous night when she had collapsed several times and her legs wouldn't support her.

Her eyes were glazed and I thought it was the finish of her.[71]

He said at first that it may have been low blood pressure due to the irregularity of her heartbeat. Her lungs weren't full of fluid and her heart rate was steady at 88 beats a minute. He couldn't throw any more light on the episode but said to call over the weekend if she dipped again. After we got home she sat looking quite innocent and unaware of the hell she put me through roughly every hour.

Despite the horror of her illness Myrtle continued to come out for day trips with me. One day we visited the home of Rudyard Kipling, the author of The Jungle Book, who had lived at Batemans in nearby Wadhurst. On a tea towel hanging on the shop wall was a poem he had written, which made me fight back the tears.

---

[70] I am always normal! Myrtle

[71] Just pretending! Myrtle

It was called "Four Feet".

"I have done mostly what most men do,
And pushed it out of my mind;
But I can't forget, if I wanted to,
Four-Feet trotting behind.

Day after day, the whole day through,
Wherever my road inclined,
Four-Feet said, 'I am coming with you!'
And trotted along behind.

Now I must go by some other round,
Which I shall never find
Somewhere that does not carry the sound
Of Four-Feet trotting behind.

Rudyard Kipling

Living with terminal and incapacitating illness, whether it be human or animal, is an open ended sorrow. Vets can only make a judgement based on their training, the animal's behaviour, pain and the efficiency of modern medicine. Her level of congenital heart disease and mitral valve failure usually results in death within eighteen months of initial diagnosis.[72] If caught early enough, then three years is rare but isn't unknown. I was so grateful to have her with me, still enjoying her life, despite the handful of daily tablets. She had such a strong life force.

---

[72]Don't believe everything you hear. Myrtle

We were off for yet another visit to Alex a few weeks later. The new tablets had brought her heart up to speed and her lungs were clear but it turned out that in my distressed state I'd mistakenly been overdosing her on one of her medicines with a whole tablet daily instead of half of one.

Beware of being in such a flap you don't read the label - I could have finished her off. However Alex the vet said continue as it obviously worked, and he didn't need to see her for a month! She RAN after me on her walk!

I would rather have had Myrtle have a happy life from A-Z than a happy one from A-S and then the rest confusion, pain and fear. I vowed that as soon as I saw her sink to a point where she didn't bounce back I would close her life while she was on the tipping point. I didn't want to keep her alive for me. I wanted what was the least stressful for her. I had lovely memories of a sweet little dog, and the greatest gift I could give her was to make the inevitable comfortable and kind. Only I could judge the time correctly. I'd know when I reached it.

About twenty more visits further on, with no further crises, Myrtle decided that Alex the vet was some form of sadistic dog torturer.[73] Every time we visited him and the words "She's doing fine", were uttered it was as if Myrtle heard them and thought: "Hurrah! More roast chicken!" And headed for the door.

---

[73] I cant imagine why else he did unspeakable things to me and forced me to take tablets.

Some days the fear made me feel sick. I'd watch her constantly, monitoring her walk, her food and drink, her expression, her sleep pattern. Nothing gave me comfort until one day from an unlikely source. I had had almost no sleep and had gone to the Llama Park for a coffee with a friend. I had been crying and it must have shown. The owner of the park came and asked me what was wrong and I blurted out about her illness and how it had gone on for more than four years beyond the time when she was given only hours to live.

The man sat down and spoke to me quietly: "My dear," he said, "Every living thing has an allotted lifespan, even a vegetable. You do, I do. It is how things work on this earth. It is the rule of nature. You can outwit it for so long but nature will win in the end. When Myrtle was born, it was her time to be born. When she came to live with you that was the right time too. Human and animal, we must all die. When she dies it will be her time to leave you and if you can accept that and not fight it, but understand that when her time is up that is because it is supposed to be so, it will help you cope and comfort you when it happens."

And somehow those words resonated with me and I clung on to them.

Myrtle with her vet Alex

Oh No not the vet again

Pub Visit

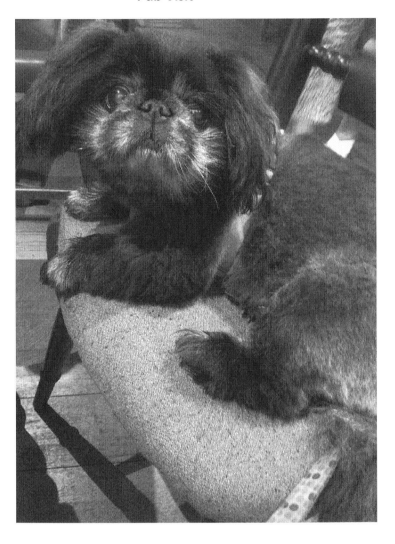

Another spring

Always uplifting

She still loved life

Chapter 10

Walks and Visits

As far as possible, weather and destination permitting, Myrtle came with me wherever we went. Many people stopped and asked her name (never mine) and greeted her happily on our walks.

People smiled when they saw her waddling along, and tiny children were allowed to stroke her. People found her name amusing and walked off chortling to themselves. I suppose they expected her to be called Fluffy or something mundane. The uniqueness of her name added to her fame and apparent personality. At least this was so until I discovered that another Myrtle lived in the village, a South African dog the size of an antelope, but fortunately they never came face to face[74].

Many pubs and cafes in England accept dogs now, even if some are corralled into a corner spot as if they and their owners have Black Death. Other places insist dog owners sit outside, which provides interesting sights in storms, snow and high winds as they sit in macs with their hoods up, trying to be jolly and eating cake and drinking tea that is getting rapidly watered down with the tempest and finally very cold too, while their dogs shelter under the table.

There is the odd officious place that gives out edicts that dogs are only welcome after 1.30 or in winter only, without giving people the option of going there at a time when children aren't running riot. Dogs are often better behaved.

---

[74]What a relief. Myrtle

One or two places completely refuse admission anywhere in or out, to dog owners with their pets. Often these are the very ones that you'd have some doubt about going into anyway because they usually look a bit seedy with suspect looking clientele. Some of the places that ban dogs have people sitting in them that look as if they have more fleas than most dogs.

Myrtle frequently had a visit to the Anchor pub in the nearby village of Hartfield close to where A A Milne wrote the Winnie the Pooh stories at Cotchford Farm. My cousin and I would have a lovely lunch while Myrtle snored under the table; visiting friends from home or abroad were usually happy to meet up there and if my daughter was over from Ireland or my son up from Maidstone in Kent, we would usually end up there for a drink and a chat. Myrtle would need to be carried in over the heads of sprawling Labradors or Alsatians who glanced up in disbelief at her furry face looking down triumphantly at them from an unusual perspective, as far as they and she were concerned.

Myrtle's excursions were so numerous and varied that to list them all would make for boring reading, but some stand out more than others. Weekly we would visit Sheffield Park gardens and walk round the lakes there; she went to Standen House, to Brighton, all over Kent, Sussex, Surrey, Cumbria, Dorset and Suffolk, visiting villages and stately homes all the way. Often it was gardens like Merriments in Kent. She met Lord Digby at his home Minterne House in Dorset early one morning as he walked his dog in the gardens there and was given an affectionate chat and greeting.

It was usually a question of "whither thou goest", unless the neighbour Joan intercepted her en route to my car, or I was going somewhere where dogs weren't allowed.

Almost daily we would walk in Winnie the Pooh country on Ashdown Forest, sometimes with the grandchildren who would sit on the memorial stones to Winnie's author, looking at the view beyond into the far distance or throwing sticks into the steam at Pooh sticks bridge. Garden centres were another favourite and visits there occurred every week. Myrtle found it too hot in summer and was not at her best. Most of our walk she would sit in the pushchair but now and then led the way along to Gills Lap where A A Milne, who wrote the stories, and E H Sheppard who illustrated them, are commemorated.

Of course, aside from Egypt, she wasn't really an international or worldwide explorer, just a local one, but my iPad obviously disagrees because it just turned the word "peke" into "Speke", the explorer who with Burton, discovered Lake Victoria in Africa in the 1800s. Burton and Peke! I like that. Myrtle discovered Lake Victoria![75]

Myrtle's outing one day was our usual one to Sheffield Park Gardens, East Sussex to be pushed gently round in her buggy, graciously acknowledging the admiration of the mere humans who were there. She posed for their photographs and would have given her autograph if they'd asked for it. She did the "convalescing from a bad heart and being ill" bit very well, looking appropriately fragile and passive. All went well until we stopped for a cup of tea in the cafe. A man brought two dogs roughly the size of donkeys to drink from the dog water bowl, next to where Myrtle was reclining. One of the dogs accidentally knocked Myrtle onto her side as it turned away.

She was instantly on her feet, eyes bulging, three remaining teeth barred and horrendous threatening snarls and bad swear words being shouted at the retreating dog. "I'll eat you alive! I'll mince you and throw you over that wall! I'll tear you to bits!" And other ruder things.

[75] I probably would have done if I'd been around at the time. Myrtle

She seemed to become airborne and twice her normal size. I hastily put her into the pushchair, as everyone had turned to see what the noise was about.
As we left the cafe she smiled benignly from side to side, resuming her role as the poor sickly creature. She should have been on the stage.[76]

Another time Myrtle, my friend Julie and I went to Lamberhurst churchyard in Kent, to see the snowdrops. I had to carry Myrtle because she kept wanting to wee on the graves. Most embarrassing. I had to keep wrestling her away and hissing threats at her. Everyone else's dog was very respectful.

As she aged she was too decrepit to run far or fast. So was I..... However the forest is relatively remote and none of the walks were near roads. Her party trick used to be to take off like a rocket and disappear into vapour for several hours.

She was the Greta Garbo of the peke world, despising photography and hating having her portrait taken. I would get fourteen photos of a black blur with three eyes, thirty seven photos of the back of her head and six or seven of her tail as she disappeared off the side of the shot. With luck and supernatural patience I might end up with two reasonably recognisable photos of a dog. Usually for every sixty pictures I got two that resembled an animal. Some were just of her tail as she disappeared off the shot. Others showed half her body as she braked just as I thought she was coming into the frame.

On any walk Myrtle moved like a snail for much of the time, stopping, examining and cataloguing every grass blade while the wind screeched past and my nose turned blue. She counted 137,896,002 grass blades one week.[77]

---

[76] I refuse to be shoved about by large ignorant dogs who think might is right. Myrtle

Before any walk she mathematically calculated the distance she was prepared to walk. Off you went enjoying the scenery and the freedom when plonk she sat down. That was it. For the rest of the walk you staggered along, red in the face and pouring sweat, carrying a lump of fur that increased ten pounds in weight for every six steps you took. Finally reduced to gasping for breath, it was as if I was holding a massive 200 lb peke and my legs were jelly and staggering.

Many of the places that welcomed dogs with open arms meant Myrtle would be mobbed by the staff and given treats and cuddles. One such visit was to the local Llama Park - hot chocolate and a cheese scone for me.

We'd been kindly taken out by my friend Marian who'd driven a long way to mount a breakout from the prison which is my flat. Myrtle was of course delighted to be amongst her adoring public once more as people jostled round her, bringing their children to stroke her, while the serving staff spoon fed her ice cream.

I sat back and watched as she extended her charisma in waves extending outwards until the entire human population of the cafe were hypnotised into coming towards her.

On the other hand, my neighbour Joan tried to bring her into hospital to visit me after one of my operations and the woman on reception there nearly became admitted herself with the horror of it.

---

[77]This is probably an under estimate. Sometimes I got interrupted and had to start again from the beginning, which when you get to 137,897,001 is a lot to recount. Myrtle

I always enjoyed going to the Village show in Hartfield. The village is on the edge of Ashdown Forest. Myrtle didn't get anywhere in the dog show. There were a huge number of entries and big dogs with long crocodile noses and in variegated colours showed up more than tiny Myrtle. They were all beautiful though. She entered the best senior section and also the prettiest face section.

Never mind Myrtle, you had a good time watching all the dogs and the stalls and the Morris Dancing and we saw people dressed as Winnie the Pooh and Tigger.

Myrtle had a miserable wet walk some mornings and would then be wrapped in a towel. She would be most displeased. The little beast refused to come back to the car one afternoon. She hated rain but that day decided it was what she has been waiting for all her life. So I'd get soaked while she inspected the grass blades and re-counted a few million of them. She had three raincoats but of course most days they were safely at home hanging on a hook in the hall. In the end I would pick her up and carry her back. She snorted and grunted the whole way.

Myrtle went to visit the wallabies at Heaven Farm with me on many occasions. We went on a woodland walk there as well but the tree roots were too much for her buggy to manage so we turned back after a while. She loved watching the wallabies and didn't want to come home. She stood on her back legs with her paws against the wire making small squeaks and noises at them as they bounded around. Some were white but mostly they were brown and they ignored her completely.

In the end I sat on a bench and watched her watching them for an hour. She had to be forcibly removed from the premises at closing time.[78]

Many years ago my cousin and I went to Leonardslee Gardens, famed for its azaleas and rhododendrons. It was a hot summer afternoon and we walked around for some while admiring the flowers and shrubs before setting off along a more deserted part of the gardens through woodland.

The path got more and more narrow and thorny, and we took turnings off left or right trying to find our way back to the tearoom. Thirsty and starting to panic as an hour passed with no sign of civilisation, we stumbled on, beginning to feel nervous as the sun started to go down.

Then suddenly before us, the woodland path opened out and there in the centre sat a white wallaby. It bounded away ahead of us, so we hastily followed it, only to find ourselves out of the wood and by the lake not far from the tearoom. It was like something from Alice in Wonderland sent to rescue us.

Myrtle had a lovely time without me one day when I was in London. She went to a friend's house and played all day with a huge sheepdog. Once home, life with me must have seemed quite boring, EXCEPT on the way to my friend's house, as I was driving on the main A22 road from Forest Row, towards East Grinstead, a kangaroo came leaping towards us along the road, coming from the other direction, pursued by an out of breath chocolate Labrador, followed in turn by about fifty cars with irate drivers unable to see what the hold up was. It was quite an original excuse to explain why I was slightly late.

---

[78]Any time we were anywhere interesting Daphne always wanted us to leave. Myrtle

Apparently there are some wild wallabies on Ashdown Forest which escaped years ago from a private estate. They die down in bad winters and then increase again over time. This was only the second time I'd seen one near here in forty years. Myrtle was asleep in the car and missed it! Apparently they'd escaped from a wallaby meat farm and were descending on our village!

August meant looking after some of my grandchildren. This meant a) Myrtle had to stay at home with the neighbour b) I would be exhausted. One London outing was on a speedboat up the Thames from Westminster so Myrtle stayed mostly at home for a boring week.

Myrtle loved being with Joan the neighbour as she had a floor to ceiling window that she could look out of and Joan also kept up a continual parade of different bone china dishes with various tempting morsels on them. Some of them did not meet with Myrtle's approval and she would try to cover them up and then sit facing Joan and glaring in fury that such frightful food could be offered to her.[79]

Myrtle and I would cat and dog sit for my daughter some nights. Myrtle was terrified that Bailey the Pomeranian would eat her food even though she didn't want it, so she had to sit watching the dish.

When the cats crept in, Myrtle greeted them with joy in her heart and was torn between food guarding and cat worship.

---

[79]Indeed. Only the best for me. Myrtle

Myrtle was horrified at having to wear her "cold coat", nice and cool and soaked in icy water, for the stifling summer heat, for her two minute wee walk. She sat rigidly down, looking as if she was posing for a sculptor and refused to even take a step[80]. I ended up having to carry her and getting so soaked that I looked as if I was sweating profusely as people passed us by.

We staggered back home with me carting along an inert and muttering Myrtle. After getting indoors she fixed me with an accusing and stone like stare.

Myrtle and I were disappointed that all the tickets were sold out for a dog friendly showing of the film "Isle of Dogs" at a cinema in London where we had intended going. The cinema provides blankets, biscuits and water for the dogs who are only evicted if they cause a commotion. Meanwhile the other dogs sit with their owners enjoying the film, presumably without popcorn and Pepsi.

I had told her about the proposed trip and just about everyone else too and had planned the journey to London and back but presumably so had half the dog owners in England because every time I tried to book up tickets they were always all gone. "One day", I vowed, "you shall go to the cinema Myrtle!"[81]

We were out for a walk in town and her adoring public mobbed her as usual when someone asked me if Myrtle was a Hairy Pug!!! Imagine, a breed as venerated as the Pekingese and Myrtle in particular being so insulted! She had to be carried back to the car. After a bad night remembering it, Myrtle had filed the woman's face in her brain for future use.

---

[80]Try wearing one yourself and see how far you'd walk. Myrtle

[81]Better still I'll be in the movie. Myrtle

Not all weathers were Myrtle friendly, even when she was clad in her little red waterproof Mac. The forest could be muddy and her short little legs could mean she sank to her armpits in mud and got stuck. Pretending she actually meant to do it did make her look a bit silly.

In fact as rumour has it, there were quicksands in parts of the forest. Once when my son was small we were down in a valley miles from our usual walk when he shouted for help. He was in mud so deep that it almost reached the top of his Wellington boots. I sensed he was sinking further and bodily lifted him out of his boots which remain there to this day.

Another story tells of a tank parked in the forest overnight during the last war and disappearing into the quicksands by morning. If all else failed I'd take her to the garden centres.

Before I went to Egypt I stayed for several months with my close friend Christine. She lived in a large house miles from the main road in a stable conversion and I was able to have a kitchen, bathroom, bedroom and sitting room all to myself. Unfortunately for me the beautiful garden was enormous but not fenced soundly enough to keep Myrtle in it.

More unfortunately still, Christine was not on the best of terms with her next door neighbour who was given to complaining about trivia. Thus it was that Myrtle developed a crush on the neighbour's dog and made her life's work a tunnelling attempt through brambles and bracken to get under the fence and into his garden to look for him.

As Barbara and her husband David were arriving to see me from New Zealand, I'd had my hair done during the morning and made myself look presentable for their arrival. It was then that I noticed Myrtle was absent without leave. The horror of where she might be flooded over me.

I rushed out into the rain and spied her through the bushes cavorting on the lawn of the enemy neighbour and barking at their back door. I crawled commando style through the brambles and sweet talked and called in vain. Myrtle wasn't budging. Finally I got under the fence the same way she had, by now covered with mud, leaves, prickles, bits of tree and soaked to the skin.

I caught her and carried her back through the undergrowth just as Barbara and David rounded the corner with Christine to announce their arrival. It wasn't the reunion I or they had expected.

Some days later I met the neighbour while walking Myrtle. She stopped me to admire Myrtle and said how her dog loved to talk to her through the fence. I nodded in an understanding way and smiled with sealed lips. After that Myrtle was tied with a long lead to a stake on Christine's lawn and never made an escape again.

We met many dogs who wanted to be introduced to her. Often these were small dogs relieved to see something near their own size but giant dogs were also fascinated by seeing what appeared to be a barking hamster approaching. She must have thought that her fame had spread far and wide.

Myrtle and I would sometimes see in the New Year at my cousin's house in Kent. She had a Persian cat called Nimbus. Myrtle loved him but he hated her and refused to play with her. She would sit wistfully watching him.

The cat previous to Nimbus was Harvey who was black and furry and when he and Myrtle sat side by side, the view from the back made them indistinguishable.

A massive fire decimated fifty acres of Ashdown forest in the spring of 2019 and reports were shown on television far and wide. Myrtle and I went up to have a look next morning as the fire had been doused during the night and was now just smoking.

For a start the reports of its whereabouts were inaccurate as it was not at the Kings Standing part of the forest but near Pylons car park, miles away and much farther across towards the road to the town of Crowborough.

Why is it that newspaper and television reporters always get things wrong? You almost expect to read things like:

"Myrtle the 57 year old white ferret belonging to Mrs Diana Constantinople, aged 22, was involved in a brave rescue attempt today on Ashdown Wood in West Sussex, trying to pull Wally the Pong out from the flames that engulfed the area".

Anyway no sign of Winnie the Pooh but I think Myrtle firmly believed we had rescued him somehow. She seemed to inflate at the scent of excitement.

After her extraordinary adventure thinking she was rescuing Winnie the Pooh from the forest fire (for which read: "me driving in the car and staring at a big burned patch of ground"), Myrtle needed a rest at the garden centre in the afternoon and was yet again encircled by admirers wanting to stroke her and to know all about her.

It must be exhausting being a celebrity.[82]

We visited Suffolk one year with my cousin driving us up there to stay in the little village of Nayland.

We walked around the villages and along the river banks and had a wonderful time and met some lovely people as a bonus, which resulted in Myrtle attending two parties on both evenings that we were there, where she was of course the focus of attention.

We could easily access Lavenham and Castle House, the home of Sir Alfred and Lady Munnings in their life time, together with their many dogs, including the amazingly famous Black Knight, the now stuffed Pekingese who looked like Myrtle but wasn't now as lively.

He had belonged to Lady Munnings in the 1940s and 1950s and became newsworthy for being smuggled into state banquets, weddings and even the queen's coronation.

The life story of Black Knight had always fascinated me. Special permission was granted for Myrtle to meet him some sixty years after his appointment with the taxidermist, even though dogs weren't normally allowed in the house where many of Sir Alfred Munnings paintings were exhibited. [83]

Nothing would induce her to react to the still silent creature before her. Dead, gone and useless was her general verdict.

However, despite Myrtle's contemptuous attitude, the story of Black Knight is so extraordinary that it is told in the next chapter.

---

[82]It is exhausting having to police the forest single pawedly. Myrtle

[83]I'd been quite excited at the idea of meeting another peke but a sixty year old dead one was a bit of a let down. Myrtle

Myrtle meets the stuffed Black Knight

The Christmas Peke

In the bluebells

Oscar the spaniel and Myrtle

At the table

Helping the TV man

Out for the day on the Romney Marshes

The Great Fire of Ashdown Forest

Meeting her toy replica

Out for a ride

On Brighton beach

Chapter 11

The Story of Black Knight, the Peke who Picked Winners

Beneath the sparkling chandeliers ablaze with light, the tiaras and diamonds of the aristocracy shot blinding flashes of prisms around the ornate banqueting table weighed down with porcelain and gold plate. Enormous floral displays filled the air with exotic perfumes. Gentle music from a small orchestra drifted across the grand scene and ladies discarded furs as they gracefully entered the huge room, their husbands in formal evening dress.

Princesses, duchesses and even the Queen herself looked for the gate crasher who was always to be spotted if one took the time to look carefully. As Lady Munnings took her seat at the table in her stunning gown and brightly coloured shawl, from under her ostrich fan peeped a small black furry face. The name "Black Knight" rippled around the table like the buzz of a thousand bees.

Black Knight was a name muttered with quiet amusement in my mother's household in the mid 1950s when I was a sensitive nine year old.

Her sisters would chuckle and when I asked what Black Knight was, I was told he was a little Pekingese dog who belonged to Lady Violet Munnings but he had now died. I thought it was sad and felt sorry for her and didn't understand why they found it funny that the dog was dead.

Mum and the aunts tried to distract me by telling me that the Pekingese breed came from China and dated back at least two thousand years. The "sleeve" Pekingese were so tiny they could hide inside the sleeves of the Chinese Emperors' ladies and his court. They were small and very furry with big eyes and fun personalities. I felt even more sympathy for Lady Munnings that her little dog had died.

Black Knight was a black sleeve Pekingese with brown paws. Lady Munnings had bought him when he was a year old despite the fact he was blind in one eye. "Well," she had sensibly remarked, "My husband is blind in one eye and he is a great painter, Nelson had one eye and he was a great sailor, so I shall not mind having a dog with one eye." She very soon became besotted with the little creature and carried him everywhere with her, sometimes in her arms but often in a bag which matched whatever outfit she was wearing.

Her husband, Sir Alfred Munnings was a renowned painter, particularly of horses. His pictures captured the movement, excitement and colour of race meetings and he become President of the Royal Academy where his work was frequently exhibited.

Of course Lady Munnings supported his success completely and this involved visiting the Royal Academy with him, which in turn meant that Black Knight had to go along too. Many institutions and public buildings do not allow dogs and didn't back then in the 1940s and 1950s either.

Lady Munnings decided to brazen it out and hid the "beyond the rules" Black Knight in his bag, cheerily breezing in time and again without admitting his presence.

Banquets and first nights became part of the exalted Black Knight's routine and he was probably the first and only dog to attend a dinner given to the Royal Family at the Royal Academy of Arts. Called 'Pudda' by Lady Violet and 'Billy Button' by Sir Alfred, the black Pekingese went to all the important functions of the day tucked away in Lady Munnings' handbag. The list included Lord Mayor's banquets, parties at Buckingham Palace, the State Opening of Parliament, Trooping the Colour, Sir Alfred's investiture, dinners and cocktails at The Guildhall, County Hall and The Mansion House. The most important occasions that Black Knight legendarily attended were the wedding of Princess Elizabeth in 1947 in Westminster Abbey, where he was hidden in a fur muff, the Coronation rehearsal in 1953 and the Coronation procession itself.

At gala dinners and exalted functions his small fluffy face would appear over the table ledge and Lady Munnings would surreptitiously feed him pieces of chicken, sips of his favourite turtle soup, even tastes of sherry (had to be Spanish and dry) and champagne. It was not unusual to see her spooning strawberries and cream from her own spoon onto his little pink tongue for him to lap up and share with her.

Lady Munnings became bolder at elite social occasions as astounded waiters and ennobled dignitaries pretended they had not noticed the fabled four legged intruder, or were amused and fascinated by his presence. If a jobsworth type made comment in an adverse way Lady Munnings became adept at dismissing their remarks or even denying that Black Knight was a dog at all, thus completely nonplussing them. It became accepted that if you invited Sir Alfred and Lady Munnings, then a third party in the shape of Black Knight would come along too. This also applied to invitations from the King and Queen.

King George VI and his wife Queen Elizabeth who later became the Queen Mother, would hold soirées and parties at Buckingham Palace. Along would go Lady Munnings in her finery with Black Knight under her ostrich fan or inside a beautiful evening bag with a small window at the back and front for him to see out. Past the flunkeys and footmen she would walk, Black Knight keeping his side of the bargain by lying low. He was the forerunner for all the pop stars and starlets nowadays with their chihuahuas in carrying cases.

The King would ask after the canine luminary as soon as he saw Lady Munnings and the Queen would stroke Black Knight and smiled delightedly. One this precedent was set, it was hard for anyone else to object to his presence whatever the occasion.

Next time there was a big gathering at the palace the King and Queen formally included Black Knight by inviting "Sir Alfred and Lady Munnings and A N Other". Lady Munnings swept in uncontested as usual with Black Knight indifferent to the fuss, in his sparkling bag.

At the traditional Lord Mayor's sumptuous inaugural banquet where the prime minister Mr Attlee made the speech of the night, Lady Munnings brought Black Knight to the reception. Calling all the shots when the dinner started, she calmly let the legendary dog out of his bag and arranged him comfortably across her knee. He went to sleep when the speeches began.

"He goes with me everywhere" Lady Munnings told reporters "Isn't he nice?"

Lady Munnings, with dog carrying bags to match her costumes, nonchalantly took the tiny peke to church, theatres, banquets and of course to the races. "He is the reincarnation of a Chinese emperor and a Ming horse" she said.

Black Knight really came into his own in the racing scene when he became known for his ability to predict a winner. In his own personal hall of fame, the phenomenal flat nosed peke was the precursor of Paul the octopus and other more modern psychic animal specimens.

Before the race Lady Munnings would ignore the rules about No Dogs, take him into the paddock in his bag and then lift him up so he could see the horses. "When he sees one which takes his fancy he makes a sort of wailing noise", she said.

On other occasions she would read out a list of the runners and he would give a small woof to indicate the successful horse.

The atmosphere would be electric as crowds of race goers flocked to the rails, ladies in hats and beautiful dresses, men in top hats. The crowd would roar the horses down the straight past the winning post and a cheer would go up as the result was given. He had become the People's Peke.

Every week the talented little creature was given 10/- (50p) pocket money to use for his bets. When he won, the money was banked in his own special account with the bookies. He was then the only animal in the world to have such an account. Word soon spread at race meetings that Black Knight was there and had picked a horse. There would be a run of bets placed on his choice as he was uncannily accurate in his selections.

People began phoning Lady Munnings to ask what Black Knight tipped for the Derby or the Grand National. Even when the odds were unlikely, the abundantly gifted small canine somehow seemed to sniff out the winner. Jockeys started approaching him in the paddock hoping that he would single them out on their mounts.

Even more unimaginably nowadays, he was seen pursuing the horses up the course at the start as the rope was lifted and "They're off!" was shouted. Soon his little legs would get tired and he would have to be retrieved by Lady Munnings. In those days people laughed and pointed him out – and no one arrested her or objected.

"I first took him racing two years ago and he has been a very successful punter. He is much better than I am at picking winners. He has his own account with a firm of bookmakers and it shows a handsome balance," Lady Munnings explained. The furry expert's bankable coups included a 10-1 shot - Freebooter winner of the Grand National at Aintree and Nimbus 4-1 winner of the Epsom Derby.

Lady Munnings explained that the winnings covered the upkeep of her incomparable little pet and also provided for the other dogs in the kennels at their country home Dedham in Essex. She had a quick answer to the question as to what happened when Black Knight had a losing day.

"Oh" she replied "his losses would go against my housekeeping account." But she assured everyone that so far she had not yet had to resort to that.

The pinnacle of his tipstering career came with his pronouncement that Sir Gordon Richards would win the Epsom Derby during the new Queen's Coronation year. Despite general anticipation that the Queen's horse would win, Black Knight was adamant that this year was to be Sir Gordon Richards' triumph. He was of course correct.

Picking winners was only a sideline for this all-knowing tiny life form whose fame spread far and wide when he was first mentioned in the columns of The Times. Afterwards, all over the world newspapers began reporting on his social activities in the high echelons of London life. He was referred to as "Sir Alfred and Lady Munnings' personal domestic deity".

Soon journalists and reporters wanted interviews with Black Knight and the phone would be ringing from morning to night with requests to drive the 65 miles from London to Suffolk to photograph and meet him. No 10 Downing Street, The Victoria and Albert Museum, Madame Tussauds, The Wallace Collection, St James Palace, The Tower of London, all played host to Black Knight.

Wherever Lady Munnings went she would be stopped and surrounded by an eager crowd asking "Have you brought the dog?" Black Knight felt obliged to peep out from under Lady Munnings' shawl to say hello, his squashed little nose whiffling as he looked out at the sea of onlookers.

For his seventh birthday, gilt edged invitations were sent out for the party. Cables, telegrams and letters of congratulations poured in all day to the grand room where he sipped dry sherry with a distinguished crowd of guests and surveyed the vast pile of presents. The main gift was a cheque for £50 from Sir Alfred Munnings. One London newspaper columnist asked Lady Munnings if Black Knight would buy a wife with the money.

"Certainly not" said Lady Munnings "he is a confirmed bachelor. He'll use it for his betting of course".

Black Knight was soon prevailed upon to write a book (ghosted by the obliging Lady Munnings) in which he set out some of his jaw-dropping adventures and the story of his cork-popping life so far in the Munnings household. The front cover was a painting of him by Sir Alfred Munnings. Called "The Diary of a Freeman", its title came into being because of one of Black Knight's more famous banquet attendances at the Guildhall.

As usual Lady Munnings arrived with Black Knight cunningly concealed and to all intents and purposes invisible. A warm speech was made to welcome all who were there but especially "a Chinese gentleman". Later in the evening such famous men of the day as Lord Mountbatten and the Deputy Governor of New Zealand made speeches and then after the health of the guests was drunk, the speaker announced "We have amongst us a gentleman from China, a stranger, an uninvited guest! I do not know if I should call him a gatecrasher or a squatter!"

To Lady Munnings' surprise and delight the "Chinese gentleman" referred to was Black Knight himself. He was made a Freeman of the City of London on the spot and had his photograph taken on the table to great applause. The honour entitled him to feed goats on the Embankment, enter public buildings and hunt polecats in St Paul's churchyard.

The amusement that this caused at the banquet must have made the evening great fun. Lady Munning's eccentricity and indulgence was not only tolerated but actively encouraged to brighten what might have been a series of stuffy or boring occasions in post war London. He really was one of a kind.

Black Knight is still the only dog to have been made a Freeman of the City of London and is seen below wearing his Freeman's badge, in November 1952.

On 26 February 1955 Black Knight died. He had dined off gold plate, numbered Princess Margaret amongst his personal friends and had met anyone who was anyone during the nine years and nine months of his life. He had seen and done things far and away beyond what any average dog would experience, even if for him it just involved the comfort of the warmth and closeness of his owner and the food treats he had learned to expect and enjoy. No doubt his horizons were much lower than those attributed to him by his fans.

Lady Munnings issued a statement: "My beloved Black Knight sighed twice and died while sleeping on my lap. He had had a weak heart for some time. I am broken hearted" she said.

She adored him and had centred her world around him. But this was not the end of Black Knight's pioneering story. He paid a visit to the taxidermist and was stuffed. On his return he continued to accompany Lady Munnings as before in his little dog carrying bags, hence the amused comments by my mother and aunts when I was a child.

There was a rumour that Lady Munnings kept in touch with Black Knight through séances. If this was so, quite how he came through and what manner of communication he used remains a mystery.

Lady Munnings' posthumous link with Black Knight tucked under her arm shocked and unsettled many people. "Morning Lady Vi" said one villager at Dedham on seeing her, "are you going to carry around Sir Alfred like that when he pops off?"

She was a regular visitor to Newmarket after Black Knight's death and descended on the shops carrying him under her arm. One of the salesladies went to stroke the dog only to find him stiff and cold which must have given her a shudder.

When Lady Munnings took afternoon tea with an acquaintance, a silent, fixed eyed Black Knight peered at them from his carrying-bag. It was only when the dog ignored the biscuits she offered him that her companion realised he long since been dispatched to the taxidermist.

She also visited the horticultural shows near Dedham, opening them and presenting the prizes, including the 'Black Knight' trophy in memory of her dead pet.

Lady Munnings regularly attended church with Toby, Black Knight's Labrador successor. She insisted that Toby knew all the hymns and encouraged him to sing them (which involved him howling, while Lady Munnings conducted to keep him in time). Black Knight, stuffed, came to church with Toby and sat in Lady Munnings' handbag on the pew.

As soon as the sermon started, Lady Munnings would bend down and in a very loud whisper say: "It's all right, Toby, he's nearly finished."

Lady Munnings died in 1971. A dog lover and animal defender, fiercely against cruelty to the end, her love for her furry friends was indisputable even if her attachment reached unusual levels. It was perhaps significant that Black Knight's one attempt at literary recognition, "The Diary of a Freeman", had the following well known dedication:

"I shall pass this way but once.
Therefore if there is any kindness
I can do to human being, or animal,
Let me not neglect it nor defer it,
For I shall not pass this way again."

Lady Munnings had no children so it could be that Black Knight was a child substitute though he was more like an extra limb. He went along with her everywhere and was simply there.

Perhaps she vicariously enjoyed the attention that he attracted - or was it just a joke, a send up to society as she could produce him at such grand venues and no one could do a thing about it.

Her foibles were tolerated with indulgent amusement and her social standing allowed her to get away with much more than an average person could have done. She encouraged the belief that Black Knight had a huge personality. This was in itself incongruous bearing in mind his minuscule size but all the more endearing for that reason. As this perception grew and developed over the years everyone fell in with it and joined in the game - from the king and queen outwards.

Lady Munnings was regarded as a dotty English eccentric. People laughed at her but not unkindly – she brightened ordinary days. Perhaps she simply just loved the little creature so dearly that she could not bear to be separated from him, either during his life or afterwards.

Black Knight is still going strong, in the Sir Alfred Munnings Museum in Dedham, Suffolk, where he may be seen, slightly worn and a bit moth eaten perhaps, but curled up with his various medals, news cuttings and photographs for posterity.[84]

---

[84]His story is a lot more interesting than he was when I met him sixty years later. Myrtle

Over 65 years old, the late lamented Black Knight finally
gets to sleep on forever in his glass showcase
at his old home Castle House,
now The Sir Alfred Munnings Museum in Dedham, Suffolk

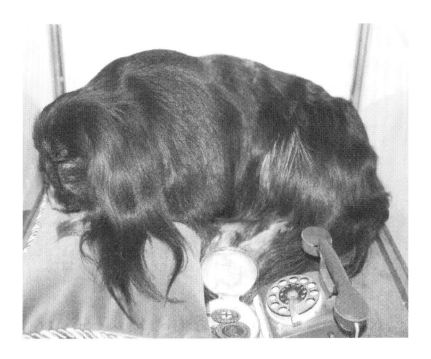

Lady Munnings and her beloved Black Knight
in his stuffed form

and when alive

Black Knight in one of his carrying bags

**Black Knight attended the Chelsea Fancy Dress Ball
disguised as a bunch of grapes**

Best wishes for Christmas & 1952
from Black Knight, misty & Violet Munnings

Chapter 12

Life in the Village

We moved to the flat in the nearby village of Forest Row in September 2015.

It was a move decided upon and instigated within ten days, which didn't make for a calm and considered time to contemplate it, but I had been offered a spacious flat under the auspices of the council, spurred on I think when they saw the photographs of the exterior and interior condition of the cottage.

I felt sorry for Myrtle, being taken away from her garden and the forest creatures, but things had reached a stage when nothing was done to keep the cottage in good exterior order (despite three separate professionally competent visitors declaring it unfit for human habitation) and this finally had defeated me.

It wouldn't have driven me out if my health had been all right but I was hurt and distressed by the constant bombardment of interference, yet with no action taken to repair or maintain the property until it became an emergency. Even then no repair ever lasted and was bodged and useless.

For nearly six years the lower gutter at the back of the cottage had been tied up with a washing line and was filled with sheered off broken tiles from the roof. My efforts to clear out the moss that slid down into it, the handfuls of rotten leaves, and cutting my hands on the broken tiles as I removed them, did not improve its condition (or mine) and water still cascaded down from it every time it rained.

Forest Row was once known as Walhatch, which interested me as my maiden name was Walls and my people had come from the village back to before Henry VIII's time. Maybe they gained their surname from the place where they lived.

The name Wal or Walls meant stranger or foreigner. Perhaps it derived from the original inhabitants who lived in the clearings of the forest in ancient times, a name perhaps given to them by the Romans or Saxons. Impenetrable, dark, dense and forbidding, the forest was virtually impassable for hundreds if not thousands of years, proving a deterrent even to the Romans. It was then known as Anderida and stretched across the whole of what is now Sussex and beyond. Brigands, cut throats and thieves lurked near the pathways and narrow ways, ready to attack any intruders.

Wild Boar, deer and probably wolves or even bear must at one time have roamed there and it was finally set out as a hunting ground for royalty in the time of John of Gaunt. To define its boundaries, am earthen bank was made around it, known as a pale.

This word pale is still used to describe something out of bounds, forbidden or impossible, in the expression 'beyond the pale.' The word first came into use around Dublin when a pale was made to discourage attack from the wild Irish tribes. Beyond the pale was a place you wouldn't want to go.

Nearby too was Whalebeech Farm where my family were tenants for some years in the early 1800s. Again the name Whale is probably derived from the same source. In the 1950s the twelfth century farmhouse was demolished for the Weir Wood reservoir, which was formed by damming the river Medway not far from its source.

On hot summers when there was no rain, the reservoir would shrink and lap against the outline of the former farm foundations. Many local properties had fireplaces and garden walls made from the stones that had once been the walls of the farmhouse.

Also revealed in droughts was the little winding lane that had led to the farmhouse and Admirals Bridge which had once spanned the small stream that was the start of the river Medway. Freshwater mussels clung to the bridge and it was poignant to see the little road still there and know it remained even under the water, wending its way towards the farm that was.

Forest Row's main claim to fame was being host to one of the last public hangings in England. In 1802 two men had robbed the mail in the village and had been caught in Liverpool in the north of England. They were tried, found guilty and brought back to Forest Row to be hanged at the exact spot where they had committed the crime. Three thousand people came from far and wide, bringing their children to watch the hanging, armed with picnics. The men were hanged from two holly trees, which were still to be seen within living memory. One presumes the children who witnessed this gruesome sight were deterred from a life of crime as a result.

In the small graveyard, opposite the church, was the grave of my great grandmother Ann Walls, nee Huggett. Her grave was just a grassy mound covered with daisies, dandelions and buttercups and little buzzing insects. There was no headstone.

She had married my great grandfather when he was in his late fifties and she in her late thirties. They had three children.

At the age of sixty five my great grandfather died of heart problems. In those days there was no help from the state. Ann had to return to the village and rent a cottage and try to eke out money earned from taking in washing and cleaning for people, in order to feed her children. Sometimes there was nothing. No money and no food. It was then that she would throw herself on her sister Jane's mercy and ask for help.

Jane had led a more single minded and successful life than her sister Ann, my great grandmother. At an early age Jane had become housekeeper for a farmer who was widowed and she remained in his service most of her adult life.

It seems she occasionally filled in for the then Earl de la Warr's housekeeper at Buckhurst Park, which adjoined the farm, because when the Earl died young, as family legend has it, she was left property, furniture and money.

I was told by elderly relatives that Jane and the Earl had fallen in love but their status was too different and nothing came of it. He allegedly never forgot about her. The evidence may be there in the vast amount of money she had stashed away, the porcelain and items of furniture that were passed down with the Earl's crest and left by Jane to her sister Ann's children when she died.

At the age of sixty two Jane had married a George Stone. This was in the days before the Married Woman's Property Act, so on marriage everything a wife owned belonged at once to her husband. This did not go down well with Jane. When, on the church steps after the wedding, her new husband asked for her bank book, she threw a Victorian hissy fit, stormed off and never set eyes on him again. When she was asked to provide money for his funeral a decade later, she flew into another fury.

Her somewhat feisty and mean temperament seems to have been recognised. When Ann approached her for food for the children, Jane pointed out windfall apples and pears in the garden. She wasn't big on housework either. When she died the family had to clean her kitchen floor with a hoe.

She came good in the end though as her possessions, property and money were left to her nephews and niece, my grandfather being the eldest, and then a station master at Forest Row. Jane's headstone in the graveyard was quite grandiose and large in contrast to her sister Ann's unmarked grassy mound.

Notably, after Jane's death, the children of her niece could be made to behave by threatening to lock them in a room with her photograph.

So Myrtle and I moved in to join the ancestors as it were, in the village where they had farmed for centuries.

Myrtle was a bit of a wuss at first if I left the flat even for a few seconds to put out the rubbish. She thought I was going for good. But we were cosy and happy when we were together there at the flat. Rainy walks on the forest, visits to the garden centre with friends for tea and cake AND she got pushed around in a trolley with the plants.

In the quiet days that followed she became good at projectile vomiting, spitting her pills like bullets across the room. In order to lay claim to the rug, she sicked up the lightly poached salmon fillet I had cooked her to spoil her a bit after the move, goodly and succulent. She chose the place carefully. It was in the middle.

Myrtle had the most amazing ability to whistle up illness on weekends or bank holidays when the vet was shut or when I had run out of money and was lying awake at night worrying about how to feed us for the week.[85] Inevitably these panic stricken visits with me tearful and terrified were sorted out quickly by Alex the vet who must have been as fed up with seeing us as Myrtle was being there.

It suddenly occurred to me one night that since I lived alone with Myrtle, if I were to be out in my car without Myrtle and had a crash, no one would know there was a dog alone in my flat. I thought of having a note tucked inside the windscreen saying "in event of accident please contact my daughter as dog is alone at home". Then I thought - well what if I collapsed in a shop. I need to have a note in my purse as well.

By now I was imaging scenarios where such notes needed leaving almost everywhere, on trees nearby, on my front door, in my car window and tucked in my underwear. I was suddenly terrified by a vision of Myrtle trapped indoors and being left there for days with no one knowing. I think the accident with the deer made me realise how quickly life can swerve off in a different direction with potentially catastrophic results.

Myrtle's life in the flat wasn't ideal with no garden and no windows low enough to look outside. She only had a view of feet and ankles. She couldn't see outside at all until a kind friend made a Myrtle perch and attached it to the windowsill. She spent hours looking out of the window at the birds and insects but had to be lifted up there and down again when she had seen enough.

---

[85]Just like to have a little joke now and then. Myrtle

When she was held captive on her perch, I managed to get Myrtle's photo, complete with eyes, in daytime - does anyone realise how hard it is to photograph a black furry dog? Usually the result is a black shapeless blob or occasionally one with glowing eyes. It was easier to catch her off guard when she was in her specially made box so she could see out of the window and pull faces at the birds and inspect the world.

I had to be careful to be close by though while she was on her perch, as if she decided to get down, she would leap off onto the back of the chair and slide down it like Eddie the Eagle on a ski jump[86].

Cleaning Myrtle's teeth while she behaved like a small Tyrannosaurus Rex, was not a task to be relished by the wimp like or cowardly. She would refuse to open her mouth and when I finally got the finger brush with toothpaste wedged between her teeth she wrenched her head from side to side and backed away.

Her teeth were a horrible nicotine yellow as if she smoked. The last dental clean at the vet had cost a huge amount and finally Alex the vet just chipped of the tartar with his fingernail rather than risk anaesthetic with her faint heart.

I took Myrtle to the forest whether I was ill or not. This was a huge martyr like sacrifice on my part as I was often really unwell. The little beast wasn't at all grateful and after about a hundred yards we usually had an argument about who was going to carry whom back to the car. Myrtle always won. Well she was a bit smaller than I am I suppose.

---

[86]There is no resemblance whatsoever. Myrtle

I always felt guilty when I looked at her wistful little face and heard the heartfelt sighs that issued from her if her expectations of the day weren't meant within four seconds of her deciding they should be.

Then after Christmas the snow started, horrible nasty stuff. Myrtle like all small furry dogs accumulated large ping pong ball sized lumps of snow on her undercarriage and chest as she walked, looking as if she had been encrusted with pompoms and was about to break into some exotic dance.

She absolutely hated the snow and sat up on her perch on the windowsill glaring at it and wishing it would go back where it came from. When it gradually melted she had a smug sort of expression as if she had hypnotised it into leaving. She was affronted by the few remaining unmelted bits.

For a while afterwards she couldn't bear to look out of the window in case the snow was still there. I felt the same. I was still struggling with a horrible virus and didn't want to go out to the park but Myrtle needed to check that the snow was melting. I think if she could have done, she would have written to the papers about the snow. She wanted it gone. She finally sat up on her Myrtle perch looking out of the window at it with a very disagreeable expression.

You could read her thoughts clearly when it finally melted for good: "Disgusting snow has now gone. I stared at it for a long time yesterday and finally intimidated it so it disappeared today. At last my favourite bits of grass and plants felt it was safe to come back. I had a nice walk in the park this afternoon without my coat. Bliss!"

Myrtle was not able to accompany me to Wembley to see my granddaughter Amelia sing solo in front of an audience of 13,000. Myrtle took two days to get round to forgiving me for leaving her with my neighbour Joan that night while I slogged up there. She sat with her back to me and swiftly turned her head away if I talked to her. I began to wonder if Myrtle thought she should have been on stage instead. "Why? Why not me singing?" Myrtle said, using her eyes to transmit the message.

A normal Daphne day followed. A lady from my apartments had to go to Eastbourne that morning but public transport would take her most of the day. She had a bad heart. So I said I'd run her down to the hotel there on the sea front. About 60 miles approx round trip in my old car.

I loaded Myrtle in the car and the lady's suitcase and off we went. We it a huge hailstorm in Eastbourne so decided against a beach walk with Myrtle. I dropped the lady at the hotel and drove home through more awful weather. Relieved to be home, I opened the car door to let Myrtle out at home and there was the lady's suitcase still on the back seat.

So back again down to Eastbourne I drove, through more rain and hail to the hotel. I ran in with the suitcase to discover it held all the lady's medicines and she couldn't do without them so had booked a taxi home! Off I drove home again leaving the suitcase there instructing hotel staff to give it to her and stop her getting the taxi.

I got back indoors at home and realised my elderly neighbour had gone on the bus to the next village to the doctor – a round trip that would take her two and a half hours minimum. So I jumped in the car and drove to the surgery in time to find her embroiled in a discussion about future appointments, some of which were to be in an even more inaccessible village so volunteered to take her for those.

Finally I got her in the car and remembered Myrtle's heart tablets from the vet[87].

We rushed round there to discover they'd given a month's supply of two types of her tablets instead just the one I'd reordered. I hadn't enough money for both so paid for one and had to return Friday with the money for the other one.

I was fraught and exhausted and ready for bed at 7pm.[88]

I got up a week or so later feeling my head was full of cement and my throat was raw. I went into the village to get medicine from the chemist. It was shut for Good Friday, so I drove with Myrtle and the neighbour into East Grinstead. I dumped the neighbour and Myrtle in the park and went to the big chemist in town where I bought anti-inflammatory throat spray, Metatone tonic and black elderberry juice. Huge bill. Then I drove back to the park, got Myrtle and the neighbour and thus back to Forest Row.

Finally I got indoors. No medicine in my bag. I'd left it on the counter in the chemist. So off back to East Grinstead and retrieved my medicines. I got outside the chemist shop to find the road closed so I had to drive right round town to escape. At last I got indoors clutching medicines at 11.30 am having left home originally at 9.15 am, expecting to have been gone half an hour.

These strange occurrences seemed to attach themselves to me all my life. My children and their friends learned many decades ago to be cautious if I took them out for the day. Things happened.

---

[87]By now I think I needed to swallow the lot in one go. Myrtle

[88]So was I. Myrtle

My elder daughter, then aged eleven, gave an accurate account of what the gunman was wearing but the disappointed policeman said nothing in my own description matched the facts. Despite this, he did kindly buy the children an ice cream each.

We walked out of the police station into a barrage of cameras and flash lights. I was interviewed for all the major newspapers and appeared on the news on television and radio for days afterwards. These things don't happen to other people who go out for a pleasant day with their children.

One morning, I drew my curtains in the sitting room only to have the whole pelmet, curtain rail, curtains, screws, bolts, plaster and dust crash down on my head! I had been assaulted by normally inanimate objects in an unprovoked attack! Thank goodness Myrtle was still asleep in my bedroom because one of the big bolts or screws could have injured or blinded her as she sat on the sill looking out of the window. Fortunately the council sent a kind man who mended it all and Myrtle safely observed life outside from her perch once more.

I was a shaking wreck all day wondering whether the Hoover would start chasing me round or the knives and forks in the drawer leap out at me.   I seem to have led a strange life whereby normally inanimate objects take a dislike to me and gang up to destroy my peace of mind.

One day I decided to tempt Myrtle to eat by making up a raw dogfood recipe. The suggestion made by a knowledgable lady peke owner, obviously credited me with skills I didn't possess. I managed to get all the ingredients except for kelp, but went ahead anyway.

Unfortunately I'd left some small plastic lids inside my mixer for some weird reason and so the whole thing gave a shriek and sent the mixture into the air all over me, the floor, the kitchen cupboards and Myrtle, who had been watching with interest but then fled and hid behind the sofa. It was in my hair, eyes and down my neck.

I managed to scrape enough together to put in Myrtle's dish but she studiously avoided it and eyed it suspiciously from a safe distance in case it decided to fly into the air again if she approached.

My reputation as a hopeless cook dated back many years. The words "fish pie" can to this day cause my adult children to go pale. I had constructed this dish with great pride using the best quality fish and presented it to them for their dinner. They stared at it for some moments before asking cautiously what it was. "Fish pie!" I trilled "Very good for you." They poked it suspiciously and then reluctantly tasted it before putting down their forks.

"You are very ungrateful children," I said huffily, putting a forkful into my mouth, before slowly setting it down on my plate and adding: "Oh well, I'll give it to the cats."

Everyone decamped to the kitchen and watched me decant the fish pie into the cats' dish. The cats rushed up happily to see what delicacy had been donated, took a mouthful each and then fled for the cat flap getting stuck side by side in it as they both attempted to escape through it at the same time.

Sometimes I'd leave the pushchair in the car by mistake and Myrtle would start off on a hundred yard walk and then sit down and look accusingly at me, so we'd turn for home. One week, we met the same lady on both our morning and afternoon walks and our pace was so slow the lady assumed we hadn't been home in between.

The alternative to the pushchair would be a walk on Ashdown Forest with Myrtle and my neighbour Joan. Then we'd go on to the little garden centre for a hot chocolate and for Myrtle to meet other dogs and their owners looking at the plants for sale.

Joan carried Myrtle some of the way and then I'd take over, until both of us felt as if we had arms like a gorilla with her weight. These walks on the forest meant she walked ten yards and we carried her the rest of the way. Anyway she seemed to enjoy the outings and was pleased to have a look around. She always loved the forest so I wanted to take her there.

She also enjoyed visits to our nearest town of East Grinstead where many of my tenant farming ancestors were buried. Many people in the town knew her from my estate agency days so she progressed along the historic High Street with a sense of ownership.

The town's greatest claim to fame was the Sackville College, a beautiful old building, now almshouses but originally a hunting lodge for the Sackville family when the forest then came right up to the edge of the town. Once they forgot their old servants had been put there in retirement and in one bad winter hundreds of years ago several starved to death in the cold. The Christmas carol Good King Wencelas was written there by John Mason Neale and when we sing 'up against the forest gate' it is East Grinstead we are singing about, though King Wencelas might have been a bit peeved at being stuck in East Grinstead instead of Bohemia.

Of an evening I would ask Myrtle if she wanted to visit Joan and she would go to the front door and sit there until I opened it whereupon she would shoot like a black cannon ball down to Joan's flat and throw herself at the door like some mediaeval ramming device.

Myrtle protected her toys by sitting on them. It stopped them escaping or having to share them with anyone. It can't have been comfortable but it sent out a message to intruders to stay away from her personal property.

My old schoolfriend Barbara from fifty five years ago was arriving from New Zealand on her annual trip one summer and I valiantly made an attempt to tidy the flat.   The largest proportion of this challenge involved tidying Myrtle's toys which were strewn around the room, cunningly placed to trip up any visitor, break a few ankles and cause chaos.

 Myrtle slept while I tidied and cleaned. This took me roughly two hours and finally, content with my efforts I retreated to the kitchen to make myself a cup of tea as a reward.

Result: within ten seconds she got every single one out again and positioned them exactly where they had been. Then she went back to sleep.

Her behaviour with a tennis ball was very strange. She would chase it, grab it with her front paws and then roll onto it. She was prepared to squash it to death if it wouldn't surrender. Ha!   So the ferocious ball had threatened world domination eh? Just watch her squash it to death! No tennis ball got the better of Myrtle!

During the heat of summer I purchased a cool mat [89]at great expense so she wouldn't get too hot and could ride in the car in cool comfort. I lifted her carefully on to it and watched as she scrabbled and shifted it onto the floor and then sat back comfortably in her usual place on her blanket.

Visits my daughter from Ireland her her younger daughter always made Myrtle the centre of attention. You could see her brighten up as soon as a visitor walked through the door, but a child, well that was the best thing ever!

Her apparent affection for me only seemed to extend to using me as a mattress. After sitting on my lap for a while, she would make for her windowsill perch behind me by putting one foot in my mouth and another in my eye to gain a grip to clamber up.

Overall though, since she was ageing and had delicate health, the flat was a better bet than the cottage, being warm and cosy, spacious and with no stairs or a dreaded cat flap. Every time Barbara was due on her annual visit from New Zealand she and I anguished as to whether Myrtle would survive long enough for them to see each other again. Year after year, panic after panic, vet visit after vet visit, Myrtle triumphed and stayed the course.

Myrtle must have missed the garden and the forest animals so I tried to take her up to the forest most days to make up for my decision that we should move. She adjusted well but I know given a choice she would have preferred to have stayed in the forest cottage despite its faults.

---

[89]This is like a cool coat but flat so you sit on it and get a cold wet bottom. Why???? Myrtle

Her nature though was acceptance and gentleness and appreciation of the people round her and the places she visited. She was the easiest of companions and the most loved.

My great grandmother

The terrifying great aunt Jane

Having a chat with the ancestors

East Grinstead

Whether her many alternative dishes were
there or not, Myrtle preferred to drink upside down

A good grandstand view

Christmas Ringlets

Piggy - her favourite toy

Practising singing

Her thunder balaclava/hat

At the local dog show

With our neighbour Joan

Chapter 12

So Near our Last Goodbye

I am watching Myrtle ageing daily now. Her little face with its large shining eyes is becoming completely white as if she is wearing a mask. Her fat little paws are no longer black but tipped with white as if she is wearing tiny slippers.

The waddling walk that would break into bounces or speed her into the distance has become stiff legged and lacking much enthusiasm. Walks now are counting grass blades and watching insects, not charging away over the horizon. Her eyesight is poor and a blue film is cast across what were once her beautiful brown eyes.

She spends a lot of time sleeping deeply and it is becoming harder to wake her to go out. Her appetite varies from refusing everything to eating everything edible in sight. She drinks a lot more water.

Mostly she wants to be close to me and looks for me if I am even in another room. Even being left with a friend while I go to order tea in a cafe makes her unsettled and I can see her looking out for me to return.

I hope the end will be gentle for her, asleep and dreaming of counting grass blades or watching a John Wayne movie and not frightening or artificially induced.

What a wonderful life she has had against the sad lives of many other animals. Better even than lives of neglected children and of sad or housebound adults. She has seen so much that humans have not, but has been unaware of that privilege.

Perhaps she does value the kindness and love that has been given to her from all who know her, and the prayers and thoughts of those who only have read about her or seen her photos. Personally I believe this is what has kept her going, together with a vet that found solutions and medicine that worked.

As for me, my life has been enhanced to a degree of happiness I have never found before by sharing it with her. She has given me the confidence to strike out and do things and go to places that I would never have managed alone. She has made me laugh, been my comfort and my companion and has made me countless friends. More than that I have loved her, and everyone needs to love something in order to be a fulfilled human being.

I hope she is in my arms when we say our last goodbye but if not I will keep her ashes to be scattered with my own when my time comes.

Then it will be when the violets appear, delicate and half hidden; when the primroses mass together on the grassy banks in Spring and the bluebells burst into their glory under the silver birch and oak trees that I will remember her most.

She will live on in my mind as I gaze at the wide and airy distant views on Ashdown Forest, the gorse bright and luminous against the grey, heavy clouds. There, like Winnie the Pooh and his friends before her, a beloved little black dog forever trots happily along the tracks amongst the wild places, through grass and bracken where the insects buzz and the birds swoop low.

She was probably the only animal that ever truly loved me.

She will always fill my heart.[90]

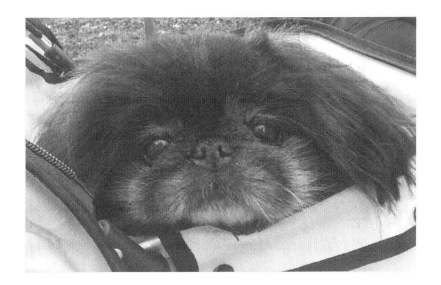

⁹⁰And you always filled mine. Myrtle

MYRTLE

How I'll miss the scraping rustles of your claws as you sit by me
And your funny snorts and snuffles as you gently settle down
And the paw I hold when sleeping
Till the morning light comes creeping
When you wake to give me reason to get up and be around.

I remember walking with you in the desert of an evening
When the call to prayer rose upwards in a myriad of sound
And the sunset turned the mountains into shades of terracotta
As we walked amongst the shadows
On the burned and barren ground.
I recall the dark of winter and the snow and ice in Sussex
And the Spring of bursting flowers and of greenness everywhere
And you patiently beside me as we made a new life slowly
With your softness and your sweetness
And your steady loving stare.

I think back on our first meeting when I knew we would be soul
mates.
How I loved your every greeting when I'd had to go away
And the hours I spend enchanted by your happy furry antics
'Til your little heart stops beating
And the world turns cold and grey.

You will go into the darkness to a place I cannot reach you
And my voice will echo emptily across the woods we've known
For the journey you are travelling we cannot take together
And adventures that you joined in
I shall have to face alone.

Through the life we shared together

And the places that we went to
You were always close beside me and rarely out of sight
But the call that you will answer is one I cannot follow
So you must pad on bravely from my arms towards the light.

So goodnight my darling Myrtle and goodbye my dearest angel.
I'll miss your warmth and closeness and your breath upon my cheek,
For this pain is overwhelming and such empty days are dawning.
But I'll see you one bright morning
My most loved and precious peke.

Daphne Constantine

List of Some of the Places Myrtle Visited

Sheffield Park Gardens, Sussex but only after 1.30 pm
The Bluebell Railway
Borde Hill Place, Sussex
Brighton, Sussex
Polesden Lacey, Surrey
Castle House, Suffolk
Lavenham, Suffolk
Nayland, Suffolk
The Pyramids, Egypt
The Sphinx, Egypt
The Sinai Desert, Egypt
The Sinai mountains, Egypt
The Cairo Bazaars
Suez, Egypt
Port Said, Egypt
The Red Sea
Heathrow Airport
The Crow and Gate, Crowborough
Gatwick Airport
The Charlwood Dog Cafe
Charlwood church
Tunbridge Wells, Kent
The Horder Centre hospital car park, Sussex
East Grinstead, Sussex
Oxted, Surrey
Epsom, Surrey
Scotney Castle, Kent
The Anchor pub Hartfield, Sussex
Shoreham near Sevenoaks, Kent
Emmetts Gardens, Kent
Standen House and gardens, Sussex
Ashdown Forest, Sussex
Duddleswell Tea Room, Sussex
Lake Windermere, Cumbria
Hadrian's Wall, Northumberland

Poole, Dorset
Wareham, Dorset
Gretna Green, Scotland
KImmerton, Dorset for fossil hunting
Athelhampton House, Dorset
Hever Castle, Kent
Romney Marsh churches, Kent
Tenterden Light Railway, Kent
The Ardingly Show, Sussex
Pease Pottage, Sussex
Aylesford, Kent
Paws in the Park, Sussex
London
Minterne House, Dorset
Lake Coniston, Cumbria
Grasmere, Cumbria
Bluewater shopping centre, Kent
Every garden centre within a ten mile radius of Ashdown Forest, Sussex
Ticehurst, Sussex
Flimwell, Sussex
Sharm el Sheikh, Egypt
Penrith, Cumbria
The Llama Centre, Sussex
The Mark Cross garden centre, Sussex
Horsmonden village, Kent
Warwick castle, Warwickshire
Keswick, Cumbria
The London Underground
London taxis
Sharm el Sheikh taxis
The church in Sharm el Sheikh
El Mercato McDonald's in Sharm el Sheikh, Egypt
Alfriston, Sussex
Littlington, Sussex
The beach at Hove, Sussex

Crawley shopping centre, Sussex
Queen Victoria hospital, East Grinstead, Sussex
Pevensey Castle, Sussex
Clouds Hill, Dorset, home of Lawrence of Arabia
Worthing, Sussex
Shoreham on Sea, Sussex
The Sussex Downs
Bexley, Kent
Greenwich Park, London
Tonbridge, Kent
Chartwell, Kent, home of Sir Winston Churchill
Westerham, Kent
Squerryes Court, Kent
Uckfield, East Sussex
Muffins tea rooms, East Hoathly, Sussex
Handcross, Sussex
Nutley, Sussex
Lewes, Sussex
Nymans Gardens, but only in winter
Heaven Farm, Sussex
St Anthony's bluebell woods
Shropshire, England

Printed in Poland
by Amazon Fulfillment
Poland Sp. z o.o., Wrocław

52500881R00169